ABDUL KUNDI

Islamic Social Contract

Copyright © 2023 by Abdul Kundi

All rights reserved. No part of this publication may be reproduced, stored or transmitted in any form or by any means, electronic, mechanical, photocopying, recording, scanning, or otherwise without written permission from the publisher. It is illegal to copy this book, post it to a website, or distribute it by any other means without permission.

First edition

This book was professionally typeset on Reedsy.
Find out more at reedsy.com

I dedicate this book to my wife Dr. Zoulikha Mouffak and daughter Ayate Mankouri.

Contents

Preface

At the dawn of the 21st century two events seem to be dominating to decide the trend for the entirety of it. The first development is the continuing economic recession in the industrialized West. This is producing civic unrest against the established social order and raising questions about the effectiveness of secular democratic institutions. The popular uprising of people to overthrow autocratic rulers in the Muslim majority Middle East and North Africa is the other cataclysmic event demolishing existing order. These two phenomena are still shaping up making it difficult to ascertain their final impact on the political landscape of the world. It is evident, the status quo is not acceptable to the majority of citizens around the world. Academics, researchers and scholars are seeking alternatives to secular democracy, especially redefining the role of religion in a social order. Islam considers life on earth as a temporary recess before a soul migrates to its final resting place in an afterlife. It offers a link connecting the deeds performed during a lifetime and salvation of the soul in the hereafter. Islam considers that the primary objective of the State is to establish an environment that not only satisfies bodily needs, but also enables a person to earn mercy on the Day of Judgment.

For the large part of the last two centuries, majority of Muslims were ruled by imperial powers of the West. During the colonial rule, the Christian majority West had tried to remake the social, cultural and religious lives of people of these countries. It can be assumed that the motive of imperial powers was to ensure the continuity of their rule rather than the promotion of Christianity. To achieve this objective, they tried to influence the linguistic tradition, distorted the history and prevented the evolution of a social order based on Islamic principles. Muslims, on the other hand, have blamed their subjugation by foreign powers on the corruption of religious beliefs and ethics. To regain their lost glory, independence movements have been influenced by the ideology to move the social clock back to the first two centuries of Islam when it was at the zenith of its power. This backward-looking attitude has dampened the desire to embrace progress in science and technology. The situation was further aggravated when Muslim modernists equated adoption of scientific knowledge with acceptance of Western culture. Conservative rural *maulvis* (religious scholars) in Northern Pakistan raise objections to allow anti-polio vaccine campaigns in their villages on the pretext that it is a conspiracy by the West to make their children impotent. To counter the emergence of conservative societies some independence movements appealed to nationalistic sentiments to secure liberation for their communities. These Muslim majority countries, even after the lapse of five decades, are still struggling to create stable social order by resolving intrinsic conflict between faith and culture, pan-Islamism verses nationalism, and to define minority and women's rights. Most of these countries, especially in the Middle East and Africa, have struggled with establishing stable democratic institutions. These failures have created a wrong perception that somehow democracy is not compatible with the tenets of Islam.

By the middle of the 20th century Muslim countries regained their geographic independence but political, economic and ideological liberation remained out of their reach. At the advent of 21st century, economic and political weakening of the West has provided an opportunity for Muslim populations to gain at least political independence. Evidence of this is the electoral success of Islamic political parties in Turkey, Egypt, Tunisia, Indonesia, and Pakistan. Manifestos of these political parties aspire to establish an Islamic Social State. However, these parties fail to provide viable political solutions that can address social issues such as acceptance of diversity, equal rights to all citizens, women's rights and containment of extremism. They fail to provide a road map that could resolve ideological differences between politically influential orthodox Islamic scholars, which are a minority, and the educated middle class that are the majority.

Human condition is evolutionary in terms of unlocking mysteries of the universe as well as understanding the divine message of a revealed religion. It is sad that doors of *ijma* (consensus) and *ijtihad* (reasoning) were permanently closed around the 11th century. Despite a clear philosophical advantage over the West in unlocking the wisdom of Greek philosophers, the Muslim *Ummah* (community) fell behind because progressive understanding of the Divine message was not allowed to prevail. This inability of Muslim scholars to evolve contemporary interpretation of the Divine message, in the light of new discoveries in social sciences, has severely affected the gradual political transformation of Muslim societies. Dynastic rulers considered it politically expedient to promote interpretation by early scholars of Islamic thought as final and infallible. To address administrative issues arising from doctrinal difference between Muslims, the *Millet* (nation) system and multiplicity of legal codes was introduced. This stalemate of thought alone can be blamed for the colonization of Muslim lands around 17th century.

Much like other fields of science and reason, Muslims have fallen behind in developing social sciences. The Muslim inability to offer an alternate system to secular democracy is the result of a lack of interest in anthropology as a science. *Sharia,* developed by Muslim scholars in the early centuries of Islam, provides a legalistic perspective to lead a life of piety and righteousness. It is not a political theory that helps design institutional structure although it can provide guidance. *Sharia* does not enjoy divine status by itself, as the Quran does, but it is a human effort to guide people about the practical aspects of the revealed message. Much effort has been put in to develop it, which mainly focuses on individual behavior, while not much effort has been made to understand the anthropological aspect to enable Muslims to organize their societies. Modern society is not purely legalistic but a combination of rights and duties that are voluntarily accepted by citizens. Failure of Muslim majority countries to evolve a social order impeded development of a political structure that is unique to their cultural and religious traditions. This produced botched efforts to adopt Western models of secular democracy.

Much like other fields of science and reason, Muslims have fallen behind in developing social sciences. The Muslim inability to offer an alternate system to secular democracy is the result of a lack of interest in anthropology as a science. *Sharia,* developed by Muslim scholars in the early centuries of Islam, provides a legalistic perspective to lead a life of piety and righteousness. It is not a political theory that helps design institutional structure although it can provide guidance. *Sharia* does not enjoy divine status by itself, as the Quran does, but it is a human effort to guide people about the practical aspects of the revealed message. Much effort has been put in to develop it, which mainly focuses on individual behavior, while not much effort has been made to understand the anthropological aspect to enable Muslims to organize their societies. Modern society is not purely legalistic but a combination of rights and duties that are voluntarily accepted by citizens. Failure of Muslim majority countries to evolve a social order impeded development of a political structure that is unique to their cultural and religious traditions. This produced botched efforts to adopt Western models of secular democracy.

Mohammad (PBUH) in his last hajj sermon advised the *Ummah* (community) in these words:

"All those who listen to me shall pass on my words to others and those to others again; and may the last ones understand my words better than those who listen to me directly. Be my witness, O ALLAH, that I have conveyed your message to your people".

This was a clear advice that understanding the message of Islam is evolutionary. No prior generation should claim to have fully understood it. To maintain contemporary freshness of Islamic ideology, think tanks, academics and religious scholars have to engage in ongoing research of its social message and underlying political order.

The objective of this book is to provide a macro level concept of an Islamic Social State in the light of the teachings of the Quran and political tradition of Prophet Mohammad (PBUH). It is by no means a final thought that is nonnegotiable. This book is an effort to offer an alternative to the secular form of democracy. The objective of this book is to plant the seed of an idea that can be developed into a fully grown tree through discussion and discourse.

The book is structured in five chapters, each dealing with a particular aspect of social and political questions. The appendix offers texts of the Charter of Medinah, Treaty of Hudaybiyyah and last sermon of Prophet Mohammad (PBUH) that was delivered during *Hajj* (annual pilgrimage to Mecca). These texts are not authenticated through independent investigation. The texts offered in the book are the most widely published versions of these historic documents. It was beyond the scope of this book to authenticate these documents. The verses presented throughout the book are from the translation of the Quran by Abdullah Yusuf Ali. The convention for verse numbers is *sura* (chapter) number followed by a period and verse number. For example, verse 33.025 corresponds to verse 25 in *sura* 33.

I pray that God help us all to establish a just society in our communities. But we must never forget that God advised us in the Quran (verse 13.011) that God does not change the condition of people until they change it themselves. Instead of relying on alien systems that were developed outside Islamic tradition, we have to develop our own indigenous systems. We should not get disheartened from the hurdles that are a natural occurrence at the initiation of a new direction. Islam makes it incumbent upon us to take an active role, rather than being passive, in our nation building efforts. This book is my humble effort to contribute towards this objective. It is not a book of religion but of political science. I don't expect everyone to agree with the ideas presented but if it makes you think, my purpose has been achieved.

I am thankful to Khaula Mazhar for editing the manuscript despite her other commitments. She is an established author in her own right with many books in publication. I am indebted to Arif Ansar for his critical review of the book. Arif is a founding partner and chief analyst of POLITACT, an advisory group focused on security, political and economic affairs.

Any errors and omissions are entirely my responsibility.

Abdul Quayyum Khan Kundi

Clovis, California

September 30, 2012

Secularism and Faith

A brief history of Social Development

Behavioral scientists agree that humans are a social species and require association with others to achieve their full potential. This interdependence enabled the emergence of a tribal society in the formative years of civilization when cavemen came down from mountains to the planes of Asia and Africa to engage in farming. In a tribal setting, members of a particular group agreed to abide by a cultural, moral and religious code that differentiated them from other tribes. These differences offered substantial enough motive to gain loyalties of new members to enhance a group's influence consequently containing clout of other tribes in the area. Archaeological finds of ancient civilizations make it abundantly clear that religion played a significant role in defining the moral character of a particular culture. Adherence to a religion fundamentally meant belief in a supernatural entity that held powers of mythical proportions that could not be comprehended through faculties of reason or logic. For instance, elaborate religious sacrificial rituals were practiced for natural phenomena like rain or drought that were supposed to be controlled by a deity. This blind faith created anxieties that were satiated to some extent by giving some tangible shape or form to the deity. Some of these ancient civilizations granted divine status to a particular force of nature like the sun, moon and fire. In a similar fashion, other cultures adopted a combination of idols and natural phenomena that formed their religious beliefs. Communities grew into towns when agricultural surpluses were traded among tribes. It was at this state of social development that we find first appearance of belief in one Supreme God appears in the recorded history. It is widely believed that Prophet Abraham (AS) was the first one to promote submission to one God, but recent discoveries suggest that idea of one Supreme entity is much older than that. Islamic sacred text the Quran proposes that belief in one God has been present since the appearance of first men. Anthropologists broadly classified these religious phenomena as monotheistic, polytheistic, and pantheistic.

An interesting corollary to consider is that throughout recorded history there was not a single dominant religion that was adhered to by all mankind. This diversity of beliefs resulted in religious wars causing devastation and misery. The Islamic invasion of Hindu South Asia and Zoroastrian Persia is well documented. Two centuries of struggle for dominance between Christian West and Islamic East, termed as crusades, are still fresh in memories. While religious wars caused devastation to mankind, they did not dampen the human spirit to improve its understanding of nature and materials. Scientific knowledge grew with leaps and bounds as diverse people came together in large towns. These scientific discoveries translated into new industries required diversity of skills that attracted ever larger numbers of people to congregate in towns, giving rise to urbanization of mankind. This urban migration eliminated the influence of tribes and was replaced by a larger community in the form of a nation state. A nation was represented by a dominant linguistic, cultural or a religious group in a contagious geographic region. A nation was held together either by coercive force of an army or a shared economic interest. This nation state needed a continuous flow of raw materials from distant lands to ensure uninterrupted running of their industrial complex. Economic interest to gain access to raw materials induced competition among nation states to occupy and colonize large parts of the South America, North America, Asia, Africa, Middle East and Australia. This resulted in the emergence of imperial powers that employed religion to affect the culture and values of subjugated people. Political motive, behind this rewiring of faith, was to ensure colonization of thought, subjecting the intellect of occupied people to the values promoted by the occupying power. An intellectually compliant population was considered politically passive towards the occupying force.

Despite coercive efforts by colonial powers to impose a universal faith, diversity of religion survived. Most urban centers were a blend of religions including Christianity, Islam, Hinduism, Judaism and Buddhism. Commercial success provided resources for the creation of research laboratories which accelerated the progress in scientific knowledge. Innovations in print and paper technologies enabled wide distribution of new findings creating a growing number of empowered individuals. These scientists, doctors and philosophers questioned the soundness of following a religious dogma that cannot be explained through logic, reason and philosophy. This gave rise to appearance of new forms of beliefs which anthropologists classified as atheism and agnosticism. Atheists totally rejected the idea of a Supreme Being or First Cause that was needed for the creation of universe thus commanding a mandate to define moral code for a society. Agnostics on the other hand did not reject the idea of a supreme God but required reasonable proofs for His existence. Until it can be proven they neither accepted nor rejected the existence of God.

The material success of the West, relied on manpower and raw materials from around the world, improved living conditions of these societies. Migrants arriving from dominions controlled by the industrialized West increased awareness of differences in culture, language and religion. This social consciousness induced attentiveness to accommodate diversity of culture and religion. Acceptance of diversity meant that it should be incorporated in the political and economic order of the society. Social architects realized that failure to do that would mean reemergence of past violent struggles, risking the comfortable lifestyle achieved by the mass production of affordable products. At about the same time Darwin presented his theory of evolution of species. To his credit, he did not reject the idea of a Supreme Being to have initiated the evolutionary process through Divine Intervention. Social and material scientists, that were already uncomfortable with accepting an unseen and unexplained God, jumped on this idea to present theories of social organization rejecting influence from an external agency. Coincidentally French revolution, sixty years earlier, introduced a republic based on separation of Church and State. These developments accelerated the introduction of popular democracy during gradual elimination of monarchy throughout the Western world.

In the early years of democracy religion continued to play a significant role but all this changed with the advent of the French revolution at the end of 18th century. It was primarily driven by income inequalities, between various social classes, of that society. French, driven by the thought of Voltaire, introduced socialist democracy where ideal of achieving economic parity between members of a society became a dominant theme. When socialism was unable to provide a viable solution, to reduce income disparity, it gave rise to Marxian Communism. Communists held religion, as an institution, responsible for wars and social upheavals. It considered religion to be a political rather than a spiritual force. Communists considered science and logic as positive forces while adherence to a religion was considered an impediment to social development. They blamed priests for devising an elaborate scheme of imposing supremacy of an unseen God, to gain political power by manipulating emotional insecurity of people. They were blamed to be on the payroll of industrial and aristocratic classes, to make masses accept their dominance to reduce risk of revolt. Communists considered that the function of a society is to provide equality among its members, which can only be achieved when personal rights are abolished for the larger good of the community. This meant that all assets and property including relationships are communal. This struck a blow to the institution of marriage and rearing of children. This considerably weakened family as the key building block of a society.

To contain spread of communism imperial powers, in the Christian West, introduced twin concepts of secular democracy that relegated religion to be an individual affair, without any role in the larger community, along with capitalism as its economic engine. Laissez Faire capitalism was enforced through the introduction of free markets keeping interference of government at the minimum. Capitalist economy was driven by profit motive regardless of the social consequences it could have on the community. During this ideological struggle between secularism and communism, two large religions Hinduism and Islam, as dominions of the Christian West, were not engaged in the debate. Majority Hindu and Muslim regions of Asia and Africa were ruled by Western Imperial powers of the Netherlands, England, Portugal, Spain, Russia, Italy, Germany and France. Political subjugation suppressed the values, represented by these religions, to a non-existent status although they had substantial following.

The secular West won this struggle of ideas eliminating communism from Russia and Eastern European countries, where it was dominant for almost seven decades. Communism has been relegated to the dustbin of human history as China, North Korea and Cuba, the last three communist countries, embark on reforms to convert to controlled socialism. The West accredited its scientific, political and economic success to its acceptance of the secular form of social order. These violent ideological and political struggles in the West resulted in two world wars consuming substantial human and economic resources. Weakened Europe could not maintain occupation of people in Asia, Africa, Australia and South America. Most of these independence movements were driven by nationalist fervor further eroding the significance of religion to unite people for a just cause. These movements culminated in the liberation of people that adhered to Islam, Hinduism, Buddhism and Catholic Christianity. These newly independent societies were not comfortable in adopting a secular model that was introduced by their former colonial occupiers. Hindu majority India and Catholic majority South America opted for socialist democracy. On the other hand, Muslim majority Middle Eastern, South Asian and African countries could not develop an alternative model and were forced to adopt a secular model that did not incorporate a moral code defined by their religion. By the end of 20th century, imperialism was replaced by multilateral organizations, like the United Nations, that promoted an idea of universal human rights that has to be respected by all member nation states. Any nation that fails to protect human rights, within its jurisdiction, was considered a risk to global peace. Economic sanctions and military actions were the tools used to ensure compliance by member states of these world bodies.

At the dawn of 21st century, advanced knowledge of materials enabled innovation of products that made geographic distance irrelevant for human interaction, empowering people to communicate more frequently with each other. High speed railways, cruise lines, airplanes, internet and mobile phones have enabled mankind to communicate with each other at an affordable price with increased speed and convenience. Simultaneously scientists have been able to develop tools that could explore mysteries of the universe with far more clarity than ever before. The Big Bang theory shed light on the creation of the Universe and DNA sequencing improved understanding of the evolution of species through natural processes. This new knowledge has renewed questions about the validity of the existence and utility of an unseen God. On the other hand, newly independent but industrially backward countries continue to define their societies in religious terms. This initiated a tug of war between the West and its former colonies. The West is promoting secular democracy as a social contract to be a necessary condition to modernize their societies. While the majority of populations in industrially backward countries feel that modernization cannot be equated with adoption of secularism. They prefer to include religion as one of the components of social structure. Election victories of Islamist parties in Middle Eastern and African countries, increasing popularity of Hindu fundamentalist parties in India and growing influence of Christian evangelists on American is an indication of the escalating voice of religion in politics. Emergence of a Jewish state supported by a secular West has fueled passions throughout the Middle East. On the other hand, a theocratic regime of Iran was a result of religiously driven revolution of 1979 overthrowing a secular monarchy. These developments cannot be ignored. It requires a fresh look at religion and its role in a democratic society.

Secular Model of a Society

A society evolves when a group of individuals agree to abide by a set of values and uphold them under all circumstances. Societies per se have no values as an entity rather it is a reflection of collective morals adopted by its members through a social contract. In modern society secularism promotes morals that need not be derived from a religious or cultural influence. It considers that human condition is universal and evolutionary. It assumes that human knowledge has developed enough to ascertain what these universal values are and does not accept dictation from an outside agency i.e. God or a religious doctrine to mandate these values. It empowers its members to adopt or reject terms of association through aggregation of opinions through an election process in which the view of the majority prevails. Although a secular society accepts that, in their private lives, members of a community are at liberty to practice a particular faith or culture. A State cannot make it mandatory for its members to a faith. In other words, societies are considered living organisms having their own identity and values which are indifferent to individual preferences or approval. These values have to be accepted by an individual, even if they are against their beliefs or cultural preferences, if they want to become citizens of a secular society. This creates an inherent tension between an individual's penchant for a lifestyle and social values adopted through the majority's recognition.

The objective of a social system is to operate as a fair arbiter in granting privileges or rights to its individual members. At the same time, it lays down expectations, from each of its members, as a condition of membership. A society where a balance is achieved between distribution of these rights and duties is considered a socially just community.

Human needs can be classified as temporal and spiritual. The objective of every person is to achieve survival at the minimum and happiness at the maximum. Survival requires access to food, shelter and clothing. Happiness is attained by actualization of intellectual potential through interplay of relationships in the form of family, colleagues, business partners and friends. The first category of needs is related to the physical self while happiness is a domain of spiritual self which is comprised of emotions and aspirations. Introduction of death creates anxieties for the spiritual self, for its survival and happiness in the afterlife, raising a specter whether success in wealth and prosperity is sufficient. That is where religion has a utility to serve humanity. Religion is an individual struggle to find salvation in an afterlife based on actions and deeds, during a lifetime, in this world.

A secular society recognizes temporal needs and strives to enable its members to maximize these benefits. Science has, so far, not been able to ascertain the nature of the soul and whether it survives after death. Although soul is the foundation stone of a religious belief, the lack of scientific evidence raises questions about the validity of an afterlife. This metaphysical nature of the soul becomes justification for a secular society not to be concerned about its well-being and happiness beyond death. Another challenge is the presence of multiple variations of faith with differing doctrine of salvation. To overcome this challenge, a secular social system concerns itself with physiological needs while it leaves the question of satisfying spiritual needs to the individual.

A secular social system is based on following principles:

1. The moral code is developed through a majority vote. It is assumed that collective wisdom acquired by the advancing knowledge of universality of human nature is sufficient to justify this approach.
2. Social Justice can be achieved through a penal code derived from social values adopted through majority vote.
3. Society will be neutral to the idea of God as Supreme Being and definer of a moral code for an individual. It would recognize the right of its members to pursue a religion of their choice without any prejudice or coercion from the State. All religions will be given due recognition.
4. Members of the community will be provided with a fair playing field to attain maximum economic benefit without any prejudice, extortion or hurdles from the State.

These principles are applied in a secular society through acceptance of individual liberty and unalienable rights of freedoms of expression, assembly and choice.

Freedom of expression means that an individual can say or exhibit anything as long as it does not impinge on the liberties of another person. For instance, nudists can exercise their practices within a specifically designated area. Similarly, prostitution can be allowed if it meets certain regulations imposed by the city. In the similar vein, a preacher can preach his religion as long as no coercion is used to gain followers.

Freedom of assembly is manifested through membership in political parties, labor and trade unions, religious congregation and consumer protection groups. A person can join a multitude of these associations or discontinue their affiliations at any time. Civic organizations cannot force people to join them but rather it has to be through a voluntary decision.

Freedom of choice means a member of a secular society can pursue any profession, join any civic or political association, or adhere to any religion of their choice. A person has complete liberty in choosing a profession as long as it meets the legal requirements of the State. For instance, a person has complete freedom to become a doctor or a strip club performer. It is the responsibility of the State to ensure that its members are not forced to make choices in their lives by any private or public sector organizations. All members of the community have to respect each other's right to choose.

Liberty of individual means that a person creates their own identity without any reference to their heritage, social status, religious affiliation or physical attributes.

Structure of Secular Government

The political structure of a secular government comprises of following entities and functions:

1. ***Chief Executive (President/Prime Minister)***: In some countries it combines both head of state and head of government into one office, for instance, the President of America. In some other countries these offices

are separate, like in England where the Monarch is head of State while the Prime Minister is head of government. Constitutionally, the head of state is the symbol of federation and represents sovereignty of the people, while head of the government is the functional head of the State apparatus. In a parliamentary democracy a Prime Minister is chosen by members of parliament while in the Presidential form of government it is usually through direct election on party basis. Tenure of office ranges from 4 to 6 years with term limits imposed in most democracies. An executive is responsible for managing revenue collection, state security, foreign affairs, fiscal and economic policies.

2. ***Legislature***: It is a body of elected representatives who have been granted the agency by their constituents to promulgate laws and regulations. In some states there is only one house of parliament for instance in Russia, Greece and New Zealand. In most democratic countries the parliament is bicameral consisting of an upper house commonly referred to as Senate and a lower house that has many names for instance Junta, Assembly, Majlis, and House of Representatives etc. Tenure of a Member of Parliament range from 2 years in the USA to 5 years in Pakistan. Members of Parliament usually do not have term limits to seek re-election. They are elected through party based direct elections in their constituency that is delineated through constitutional demarcation of districts. In many countries a certain level of the population is granted a seat in parliament. In the United States of America (USA) congressional seats are allocated to each federating state based on their population with the condition that each State must have a minimum one seat. In Pakistan each National Assembly member approximately represents a population of 550,000 citizens. In Indian Lok Sabha (parliament) the formula for allocation of seats is such that the ratio of seats to population is approximately the same for each federating State.
3. ***Judiciary***: Judiciary, along with executive and legislature, is considered one of the three pillars of a modern democratic system. The constitution has to ensure that Judiciary should be free from any influence of

legislative and executive branches of the government. It is upholder of the constitution and adjudicator among citizens. In some countries judges are given lifetime tenure, for instance in the USA while in others they have a definite tenure of office. Judges, in most countries, are nominated by the Executive while in some countries they have to be approved by the parliament before they can take oath of office. During their term in office judges are supposed to be beyond the influence of government to impart justice.

4. ***Provincial/State/Country Government***: In large countries, a layer of local government is introduced that has many names. For instance, it is called a provincial government in India, Pakistan while in USA it is termed as States. Union of these provincial governments forms a federation or a nation state. In the Presidential form of government, provinces are governed by Governors directly elected by the constituents registered in a State through party-based elections. In Parliamentary form of government, governors are appointed by the head of state to represent the interest of the federation while Chief Ministers are elected by members of provincial parliament to run the government as an executive. Members of provincial or state parliament are elected through direct elections on party bases. States/Provinces have their own constitutions that have to operate under the auspices of federal constitution. In case of a conflict or overlap, federal law gets precedence over provincial law and constitution. In this multilayered government there is a constant struggle between Federal and Provincial/State governments to expand their influence.
5. ***Local Government***: These comprise of mayors and city council members. Their mandate covers managing local municipalities and towns to provide community services including water, sewage, firefighting, police, local roads and garbage collection. In most countries, they collect local property taxes to fund their operations. They are usually elected through direct non-party-based election. These officials are in most cases elected for tenure of a two-, three- or four-year term. Term limits are imposed in most democracies.

6. ***Government bureaucracy***: These are career officers to perform functions according to the policies, rules and regulations passed by the executive, legislature and judiciary. These are permanent functionaries that are deferential to the elected representatives of the people. In federations, it comprises of two layers of bureaucracies i.e. provincial/state and federal each operating according to their mandate. This multi layered bureaucracy creates operational delays, duplication and financial wastage.

Heads of state, head of government and legislature are elected through a process defined in the constitution. In most countries, elections for executive and legislative branches of government are held on a political party basis. Political parties perform the function of aggregating support for specific ideologies to nominate candidates that contest elections. Aspiring politicians join these organizations, according to their ideological preferences. One advantage is that using the platform of a political party restricts policy choice to a handful making it possible to achieve compromise. Politicians have to campaign for the policy option chosen by their party even if they don't agree with it. In developed countries the process of party nomination is based on participation from registered voters which is in accordance with the democratic ideal. In less developed countries democratic this tradition is not well established. In these countries prospective candidates are nominated by office bearers of political parties which do not represent an ideal approach to democratic principles. India, an emerging South Asian regional power, offers a good example of party nomination while USA, with a highly developed democracy, provides a good example of nomination of candidates by people.

Critique of a Secular Social Contract

Unlike plants and animals which do not have highly developed intellects, humans as conscious beings have to carry moral obligations from the day they are born, as they are born into a family and relations. Birth is a social contract in which parents agree to impart their social, cultural and ethical values to their children. Besides that, parents ensure protection from disease and provision of nutrition during the years of infancy. They also develop an elaborate training program to introduce culture and tradition to a child. Their aspirations to do that are twofold. First is the continuation of their family heritage. Secondly, they have more confidence in these values because of their own lifetime of practice. All of us, in return, are obligated to take care of our parents in their old age.

In secular social system parents are custodians of a child as long as they are considered fit to discharge that responsibility. If the State feels parents are failing, it has the right to take the child away from their biological parents to entrust them to foster parents. This is contrary to human nature as children are bound to the history of their parents not only biologically but psychologically and behaviorally as well. This is now proven and substantiated by modern research conducted by behavioral and genetic scientists.

In an idealistic secular society parents should not teach cultural and religious values to their children. These decisions have to be relegated until a young adult, who has freedom of choice, freely exercises his right to choose a religion. This attitude will be in conformity with the basic right of choice granted by a secular social system to its citizens. In a way that means that in a secular conception a person is born free from entanglements of their family history and can make their own choice of an ethical code. The secular moral code available to a citizen is based on the most basic human nature while ignoring religious heritage which could provide links to the past. If a person has to refer to the past, then that would mean that they owe their moral obligation to the first creation which is the domain of an almighty God. This would suggest that a natural social order has to give due consideration to faith to develop a moral code that is true representative of the human condition. Ironically a secular state does not consider faith to be an important building block of human character. This ideology of the State's indifference to religion is reflected in the educational programs developed in most secular countries especially European nations. Parents, at their own initiative and expense, may decide to inform children about a particular faith. This isolation of faith, from an interactive and collaborative environment of academic life, has a profound effect on a person's approach to God. It is probably because of this reason that in most European countries attendance in Churches, Mosques, Temples and Synagogues have gone down substantially as the utility of religion to provide a moral benchmark is ignored. Another consequence is the weakening of faith mandated social institutions like marriage between a man and a woman, conceiving children in wedlock and assuming responsibility of old parents.

In Secular Social Order there is no room to accept the influence of culture. In other words, humans are considered as mechanisms or organisms that have autonomy of action in terms of their physical aspirations to achieve quality of life and profession. Secular society offers its citizens a set of rights that are largely concerned with material well-being. These rights have to be mutually respected without concern for the spiritual contentment of each other. People do not have the liberty to project their spiritual and emotional aspirations onto communal life. Secularism projects the idea that individuals, that are intrinsically self-governing in their choices, can come together to form a society purely for the pursuit of material gains. They engage in transactions without any desire to share intangible values with each other. For private consumption, individuals can pursue a culture for self-satisfaction as long as they don't impinge on the liberty of others. This is against basic human instinct; a natural community evolves when people are allowed to inform others of the values they believe in, especially those that are emotionally close to them like family, friends and colleagues. This attitude of limiting citizens to actively share values with other members of society is anathema to human nature which is intrinsically inclined to build communities. Secular insistence on exclusively maximizing tangible benefits would leave no room for the development of emotions of nationalism, patriotism or loyalty. It is because these affiliations are based on emotional attachment to a particular culture and tradition. Absence of these emotional bonds of community building could result in destruction of the order in times of economic and social distress. In such a society greed eventually supersedes all other human emotions and relations.

In a secular ideal maximization of happiness is related to the quantifiable benefits without much regard to emotional satisfaction that cannot be measured. It is assumed that assurance of equal access to tangible benefits will translate into emotional and spiritual satisfaction. There is hardly any example available, when a case is filed by a citizen in a court of law, seeking compensation for an emotional loss unless it can be proven that there was an accompanying material loss.

Secularists suggest that the inability of men to contain their ego, probably emanating from a tribal background, to use coercion to promote their particular brand of faith or culture is one of the main reasons for emergence of secularism. This inability of men to contain their impulses cannot be blamed on the fault of religion or culture which has largely been a positive force to shape a society. Even animals and plants have a particular culture and none of them try to impose it on the other. So, if we say that the success of animals and plants can be attributed to being secular that may be true, but we can't expect men to behave like them as it would make human society static, unimaginative and non-productive. Cultural creativity, resulting from the competition of ideas, has played a critical part in human evolution and it has to be fully recognized in a social order.

Economic prosperity and scientific success of secularist countries has created a myth that these achievements justify acceptance of a moral code developed through the collective wisdom of community. Introduction of new laws to seek changes in social values are included on the ballot paper and ratified through majority votes. For instance, in Western secular democracies homosexuality is increasingly accepted as a social norm because of a majority supporting it. This is not the first time in human history that same sex relations have been made the norm rather than an exception in a society. The Quran informs us that the community of Prophet Lot was engaged in the same behavior. This is an example of another contradiction in a secular social model, which prize itself to be driven by reason and logic, that an unnatural social relationship has been accepted. It is ironic that similar argument of irrationality of religions is used to reject its influence in matters of government. It is considered a taboo to debate a social value from the platform of religion even though all sects may agree on it.

A secular society, since it does not recognize an afterlife, does not offer a solution that can ally anxieties that might arise from injustices that remain unanswered. It projects that a social contract expires at the event of death upon which a person's right to have a recourse to justice is given up. This conversely means that a person seeking justice has to give up that right if the defender dies during arbitration. Apart from that there are many injustices committed in the normal course of life that are undetected or unreported by a system. For example, underpayment to labor, prejudice practiced by a manager, racial discrimination etc. No human system can guarantee that these injustices will not occur. Revealed religions present an idea that there will be a Divine court in an afterlife where justice will prevail. This idea of an inescapable Divine justice, applied to all without discrimination, offers hope that has to be incorporated in a social order for it to be stable.

The secular system of government presents an outside agency developed by the community, in the form of a constitution, to offer a set of values applied to the community. For instance, the American constitution claims its objective is establishment of a society that offers; protection of life, liberty and pursuit of happiness. This same principle of an outside agency is applied to other forms of associations as well. Freedom of association allows people to form commercial corporations that have their own identity, role and responsibility. A white-collar crime committed by a corporation makes the organization liable while the managers themselves may or may not be penalized. Similarly in government the Chief Executive of the government or head of state has immunity from prosecution during their term in office because government is considered an outside agency separate from an individual. This is another weakness of a secular model which has the potential to create conflict of interest between various roles of an individual rather than harmonize them.

In a Utopian secular society, once an individual is elected to public office, they have to give up their religious and cultural practice during their term in office. It is important to place this restriction because continuing these associations could influence decision making of the elected official with a particular bias towards their own religious group. Similarly, for a secular electorate, religious affiliation of a politician should not be a factor in their voting decisions. But in reality, that is not the case. Religious affiliations of a politician do play a key role in convincing voters to choose. In the 2008 Presidential elections in America, opponents of Democratic Party candidate Barack Hussein Obama raised doubts about his commitment to Christian faith and presented him as a Muslim in disguise. Similarly in Germany Christian Democratic party is proud of its Christian roots. In 2012 Presidential elections, the Mormon affiliation of Republican Party candidate Mitt Romney has raised questions about his electability. If religion is a factor in elections, then it is unnatural to assume elected leaders will not be inspired by their religious affiliations to make political decisions. There are many chaplains and priests employed by Western militaries that are paid by the secular government. Another example of continued influence of religion on secular societies is the oath administered to naturalized citizens in America which ends with declaration to be one nation under God. Similarly on American currency notes it is stated that "In God we trust". In Europe, the French parliament passed a bill which prohibited use of *Hijab* (veil) by Muslim women in public places. This law is a breach of the secular value of freedom of choice which should allow an individual to have liberty in the choice of a dress. Swedish government did not allow construction of mosque minarets because it would raise emotions in the society. This is surprising since providing complete freedom of expression is an impregnable right of individuals as well as freedom of association and assembly. It is quite evident from the preceding examples that secularism cannot survive for long until it finds a solution to bridge the gulf between individual adherence to faith and its effect on political and policy decision making.

Democracy as a tool of secularism is exercised through political parties, which has created ideological divisions within these societies. Ironically a person elected to US Congress on a platform of the Republican Party has to serve all the constituents regardless of their political leanings. Although during the nomination process a candidate seeks support of their party members but once elected, he may compromise on those values to serve the community at large. This creates an inherent conflict of interest that may be abated to some extent but remains subtly prevalent in all decision-making processes. Consider the debate on abortion among politicians in America. Republicans are anti-abortion while Democrats are pro-abortion rights. This means that a Democrat elected in a substantial Republican constituency has to be watchful of his anti-abortion position to maintain his chances of re-election to the public office. These conflicts create divisions that remain even after the elections are over. This can result in a political stalemate on key policies that develops systematic risks to the long-term continuation of a social order. Secular governments in Italy, Greece, Britain, Spain and America have experienced political deadlock on key economic decisions that initiated recession during first decade of the 21st century.

In a secular democracy, a candidate competing for an office has to reach out to voters through elaborate election campaigns to convince them to vote for their political agenda. To finance these operations, candidates have to raise election campaign funds through donations. This becomes a breeding ground for vested interest to have an influence on public policy which in some cases can be detrimental to the majority of people. In less developed countries politicians spend their own money on election campaigns. To recoup these funds, they engage in corrupt practices after assuming office. To have an appreciation of this point two pertinent examples are the United States where a member of the House of Representative needs around US$500,000 (in 2012 dollars) to run a successful election campaign when the per capita income, in the country, is close to US$27,100. The other example is Pakistan where some hotly contested election campaigns can cost candidates US$250,500 (in 20102 dollars) when the average household annual income is around US$1200. This high income to campaign finance ratio discourages many eligible and qualified candidates from seeking public office. This financial hurdle develops elite mentality and emergence of a political class especially in countries with low civic participation in politics.

In many countries voter participation in elections has been steadily going down. According to Wikipedia, an internet encyclopedia, voter turnout in the United States, Switzerland and India has been 48%, 54% and 58% respectively. Since votes polled are split between winner and losers, it means that parliamentarians are elected without a majority mandate. Candidates winning Congressional elections in America have to secure 50% plus one vote which translates to 24% of total votes polled when the voter turnout is 48%. In 2012 French presidential elections 80% people voted for the two candidates in a runoff election in which the winner secured 51.4% of total votes polled. This translates to approximately 41% of total registered voters which makes the new President democratically ineligible to run the country because he does not have the majority mandate. In a country where first pass the post system of elections is in use the percentages of polled votes secured by winners is even a smaller percentage of total voters. A long-held belief that democracy is a government for the people by the people is not necessarily true in most cases.

Another hurdle that makes secular democracy ineffective is the division of parliament into treasury and opposition benches. This creates divisions within a legislature that has to draft laws that are applied to the whole community. It is against the vested interest of the opposition to agree with the political party in power unless they can get some compromise that serves their political interest. Instead of debating on the merits and demerits of a law by itself, these parliamentarians protect the narrow interest of their political party. The sense of insecurity of losing party nomination, in case of defiance, and a desire to defeat the party in power are so strong that it is unrealistic to assume that parliamentarians will give preference to national interests at the cost of their own good. It is for this reason that constituents behave cynically when a politician makes a case for his policy position, because it is very difficult to ascertain the altruistic intention of their representatives.

The secular social contract is presented as a system that can be adopted and applied universally but the conduct of the secular democracies shows a duality of values. A moral order should have uniform application not only inside a state but also in their dealings with other countries. There have been numerous instances when secular governments showed disrespect for human rights and rule of law, which were integral parts of their constitutions, in the name of protecting their national interest. Theoretically these breaches of social justice, in dealing with other nations, should have produced mass protests and overthrowing of governments but in reality, the majority supported these acts. International media has reported that American unmanned drone strikes kill innocent citizen in pursuit of alleged terrorists which is in violation of United Nations charter as well as disrespect for human lives. The State in a way acts as a judge, jury and executioner. But the similar tactic of disrespecting civilian lives to apprehend a criminal cannot be applied by a local police officer. To seek access to natural resources Western secular governments, justify their collaboration with an autocratic ruler that blatantly violates human rights. In pursuit of economic gains wars are imposed on smaller nations without provocation or proof of violation of international laws. These attitudes are promoting international anarchy rather than developing a balance of power among nations that is critical for world peace.

There is a myth promoted that societies that adopt secular democracy are more peaceful and have contributed towards improved relations between States. It is believed that secular democracies are better equipped to settle their differences through diplomacy rather than resorting to wars. This is a misplaced conception, in a way projecting ideals of domestic co-existence outward without empirical proof. In reality, incidents of wars have not subsided in the last hundred years when democratic form of government became more prevalent among newly independent states. Since the advent of secular democracy humanity has experienced two world wars costing millions of lives as well as numerous inter-state conflicts. The sole use of nuclear weapons was approved by a secular democratic government to bring an adversary to its knees. The prime mover of foreign affairs of a secular state is to safeguard the interest of its citizens. To achieve this objective, it may adopt policies that in some situations may be contrary to the values of social justice, humanity and tolerance that are upheld inside its own jurisdiction.

These contradictory interpretations of standards are creating pressures on the legitimacy of secularism. It is this greed of domestic or national interest preservation that motivates a secular society to engage in unjust practices of accepting collateral damage of innocent lives in drone strikes; declaration of war against a perceived enemy without provocation; form alliances with dictators that oppress their people; and imposition of economic sanctions on other nations without regard for human tragedy. Self-interest is so overriding that a secular society does not feel a moral remorse when engaged in these policies. The introduction of global social networks is exposing these hypocritical actions and exerting pressure on secular systems to change.

Islamic Concept of a Social Contract

Throughout recorded human history religion has played the roles of universal arbiter of moral ethics; soothed spiritual anxiety arising from injury and death; and offered recourse to social injustice through the idea of a divine justice in an afterlife or in some religions through reincarnation to get a second chance. In all civilizations, whether tribal or urban, religion has been a potent force. Religion offers salvation of the soul, in an afterlife, through expression of righteousness during temporal existence. Secularism, maintaining a utilitarian view of religion, rejects faith in matters of State as it is only concerned with serving earthly life while being indifferent to an afterlife. Religion, on the other hand, demands a voice in defining the pattern of social organization so that it can prevent endorsement of policies, by State, that could harm redemption of the soul. Faith does not just grant a spiritual connection with the Creator but also provides a social force that keeps societies moving forward.

The Quran talks about the responsibility bestowed on men at the time of creation in the following verse:

*(**Verse 33:072**) We did indeed offer the Trust to the Heavens and the Earth and the Mountains; but they refused to undertake it, being afraid thereof: but man undertook it;- He was indeed unjust and foolish;-*

Following questions emerge from this verse:

1. What is the nature of "Trust" this verse is referring to?
2. Did Adam have an option to say No to accept the trust?
3. Does every child born carry this trust?

To find answers to these questions we have to refer to the story of Adam and his time in heaven. During his tenure in heaven Adam had the intellect and free will but he did not have the need to create. In his pure form he did not have a need for a career so there was no opportunity for thought either. During his adobe in heaven, he was instructed by God not to touch or taste a particular tree. But he transgressed that limit. For this transgression God had to punish him as demanded by the attribute of justice. The Quran tells us that Adam repented and asked for forgiveness so that he can be reinstated to his adobe in heaven. It was during that time that the question was raised whether Adam was able and willing to carry the trust to reside on earth as a creature that had the ability to be creative enjoying command of his environment but at the same time is thankful, subservient and just. It was this creative trust that God asked men to carry for his transgression in heaven and when he was instructed to go down to earth. The challenge for men was to carry his creative ability in a manner to gain salvation for the soul in hereafter. The covenant agreed to for accepting the trust was that, to help men, God promised to send guidance in the form of revelation and Prophets.

It is this ability of creativity which affords men to have command of his environment and act on it. The term *Khalifa* (vice-regent) manifests itself in this creative trust. Some scholars have attributed the "Trust" mentioned in verse 33.072 refers to intellect while others have considered "free will" to be it. Intellect cannot be the "Trust" bestowed on men because it is passive unless an intuitive thought seeks a purposeful act from it. "Free will" also needs an agency to manifest itself as a cause to have an effect. Without a creative purpose, the action of "free will" does not have any meaningful consequence. Creative ability, on the other hand, is an interplay of free will, intellect and thought pushed forward by the desire to regain the pure or original form.

No other creation was willing or ready to accept this trust because they were not sure they would be able to use that ability with justice. No other creation could create music, paint, or develop spacecraft to go to mars. No other creation could create tools and equipment to make their life comfortable, scale mountains and steer ships on high seas. The Quran often refers that these attributes were granted by God, but it was the creative ability of men that he was able to use it.

But men are unjust and foolish because he is not able to use this creative power to its meaningful benefit which is to gain salvation at the end of this temporal life. He gets sidetracked by seeking power and wealth in this temporal life as if he is an immortal. In all its endeavors i.e. politics, science, religion, arts and business, men fail miserably. In politics we are not able to create a society that is just and where we can ensure that no one sleeps hungry. We are not able to create a society where people could be rich and poor, but they still respect and help each other without getting into a class struggle. We have tried socialism, communism and secularism but none of these systems have succeeded.

The above explanation of human fallibility seems fatalistic and pessimistic. Verse 33.072 in a way is some advice to men that they must realize that they can't carry the "Trust" alone without submitting to God and seek his help and guidance at every enterprise of life. This is what Prophets realized at the end of their meditation to find God and his message. At the conclusion of their spiritual journey, they declared that they lay their trust in God alone. That did not mean that they retraced from life and became recluses. They remained active reformers within their communities but sought God's mercy in whatever they did. That is the total submission and that is the message of Islam. It is for that reason second Caliph Umar would frequently mention to his advisors that whatever good decisions he makes are from God and all bad decisions are his fault. As a companion of Prophet Mohammad (PBUH), he fully understood the limitations that are intrinsic to the human condition. In a political context verse 33.072 advises men to derive social values from the Divine revelation presented in the Quran.

The objective of a social order is to strike a balance between the rights *(huquq)*, duties *(faraiz)* and limitations *(hudud)* of its citizens. The rights of one citizen could define the duties or limitations of the other. When rights outweigh duties or vice versa it creates an imbalance that ultimately results in the destruction of a society. In an Islamic State people do not have limitless liberties but are required to stay within the boundaries proposed by the Quran and *Sunnah* (tradition) of the Prophet. For example, conceiving children out of wed lock is not an acceptable behavior. Secular societies also limit the behavior of their citizens through a constitution, but those boundaries are defined by a majority rule rather than a Divine mandate.

In terms of number of followers, Islam, Christianity and Hinduism are three large religions representing almost 80% of world population. Islam and Christianity, being monotheistic faiths, share many commonalities because they belief in one God and the Prophet Jesus (AS). Hinduism, on the other hand, is a polytheistic religion with plethora of gods and goddesses symbolizing various attributes of a supreme being. Among all existing religions, Islam is the only faith whose religious book is intact in its original revealed form even after a lapse of fourteen centuries. It is unfortunate that Christianity, the largest revealed religion in the world, has lost its original scriptures depriving humanity of its wisdom. The Bible in its current form was compiled after almost two hundred years of the ascension of Prophet Jesus (AS) to the heavens. This places Islam in a unique position as compared to other religions. It proposes social values, for its adherents, which link their temporal life with an afterlife as a continuum without a break.

Existence of one supreme God, in Islamic conception, has a social characteristic to it. Believing in One God liberates the soul to be independent, in its thought and actions, without being subservient either to a force of nature, a helpless idol statue or another human being. The acceptance of one God unifies the mankind that has the potential to arrive at divergent conclusions of a Divine Presence. God, the creator, understands that it is in the nature of men to deviate from a true path. He warns those contemplating injustices of a severe punishment. This coercive force is similar to a State, to alleviate human propensity to deviate from a righteous path of salvation.

A person can arrive at the conclusion of the oneness of God independent of any influence from a monotheistic faith. But the entry to the brotherhood of Muslims is only gained through accepting the *Kalima* (word) of Islam which is:

Translation: "*There is no God but Allah, Mohammad is the Messenger of Allah.*"

The first part of this *Kalima Tayyabah* (or pure word) is a person's faith in one God but the second part is an agreement to enter into a social contract to pursue a life according to the message of the Quran. By accepting Prophet Mohammad (PBUH) as the messenger of God a person agrees to the social contract that was revealed to him in the form of the Quran. It is because of this reason that the foundation of Islamic Social Contract is based on twin pillars of the revealed Divine Message, the Quran, and *Sunnah* (traditions) from the life of Prophet Mohammad (PBUH). The Quran provides the theory while the life of the Prophet provides practical demonstration of those values in real world environment. Prophet Mohammad (PBUH) became a living example of the teachings of the Quran both in terms of spirituality and the social values of a society. After death of the Prophet, various interpretation of the Quran became the reason for emergence of various doctrinal sects in Islamic communities. None of these sects disagrees about the validity or content of the Quran elevating it to become a uniting factor.

The objective of an Islamic Social State, as presented by the Quran, is to enable individuals to lead a life of goodness expressed in actions not only towards their souls and their family but also towards other members of the community. The fruits of this righteous behavior produce rewards not only in this world through establishment of a just society but also in an afterlife where the soul has the final resting place. In Islam people are differentiated, in rank and status, only based on their righteous deeds alone. A person is required to be concerned with his own deeds without the grant of an authority to force others to follow in his footsteps in matters of faith. Members of an Islamic Social state are expected to oppose oppression and injustice, that may be present, not only through words but through action by cooperating with the State to apprehend the oppressors to be brought to justice.

An Islamic Social contract is based on following principles:

1. The moral code of society has to be within the ethical boundaries mandated in the Quran.
2. The State should strive to establish a just society without any bias towards its members based on their religious, ethnic or linguistic affiliations.

3. Individuals are provided with an equal opportunity, but their endeavors must conform to the moral code adopted by society.
4. The State exists to serve the temporal needs and spiritual uplift of its members

These principles are implemented through following freedoms granted to the citizens:

1. Freedom of religion
2. Freedom of speech
3. Freedom of association
4. Almighty God has granted each individual, regardless of whether they believe in Him or not, the status of *khalifa* (vice-regent) on earth. This means that each person is born free and has complete freedom of choice.

The status of *khalifa* on earth is liberation, of a person, from all artificial bounds imposed by a society in the form of monarchy, idolatry and aristocracy. Islam does not recognize classification of a community based on profession, wealth or lineage. A child is born with his own unique potentialities and has the right to move between social classes based on his abilities, intellect and achievements.

The Quran emphasizes that the human condition is evolutionary. Each generation is expected to use their intellect and contemporary knowledge to build upon the culture and traditions that they have inherited. In the absence of this approach the universal message of Islam will be stuck in a bygone era and become incoherent with social needs of contemporary times. The Quran instructs all believers not to blindly follow the traditions of their parents. They should engage in their own efforts to reflect on the message that they may have a better understanding of it than the prior generation. Islam as a religion is concerned with well being of an individual in his various roles in earthly life. A person will be judged based on their adherence to the Divine mandate in these roles. To elaborate further, a person will be judged for his actions as an individual, a member of a family, and a community. For example, if a person was a son, brother, husband, grandfather, judge, and neighbor, he will be judged for all these roles.

In a Muslim majority community, it is expected that individuals will practice Islamic tenets in their daily lives. This individual behavior will project into a collective conduct helping in establishing an Islamic social order. From this perspective the objective of a just social order can be achieved by guiding an individual's actions rather than branding a society with faith. Adoption of the Quran and *Sunnah* of Prophet Mohammad (PBUH), as the primary sources of constitution, in a Muslim majority country does not make her a truly Islamic social state unless citizens are expressing those values in their daily lives. The preferred path for establishing a social contract as outlined by Islam is that people in a society will adopt it by a free will, regardless of if it is expressed in a constitution or not. Islam encourages social interaction between its members by encouraging congregational prayers in mosques five times a day as well as performance of Hajj once in a lifetime. During the Hajj people of different cultures, from all over the world, have an opportunity to come together to know each other, share experiences and collaborate as one *Ummah* (community).

Islam recognizes the human condition that they will evolve into various cultural groups. Each culture will preserve their own unique identity expressed in cuisine, fashion, rituals and language. From an Islamic outlook a unique culture can exist in harmony with will of the Creator if it does not cross the boundaries of behavior mandated by the revelations in the Quran. For example, cuisine cannot include pork or alcohol. In a diverse society Islam recognizes cultural affiliations but instructs members of each group to be compassionate towards other groups. If a dominant group is present, then it should uphold the universal values of humanity, justice and freedom. It achieves this objective by recognizing an ever-enlarging circle of influence of a person starting from a family moving up to a neighborhood and then to a city and State. At each level the individual is a driver imbibed with a universal moral code, ethics and values offered by the religion.

Islam does not consider society to be a separate entity with its own separate identity and values but presents an idea that a group of pious individuals evolve into a just society. A good society is a direct consequence of the righteousness of its members. Islamic ideology does not accept the concept of state as an outside agency which is an aggregator of values as projected by the secular form of government. In Islam a society emerges when a diverse group of people agree on a minimum agenda, offered by a shared religion, to form a community. This in secular terms can be termed as a State being subservient to religion. State derives from religion rather than dictates to it. In Islamic concept, State is an administrative unit without an overriding identity of its own. Unlike secularism, it does approve of the social role of cultures and formation of diverse communities that can live together with peace and harmony. Individuals are expected not to discriminate among each other based on ethnicity but intermingle through marriage, business partnership and community organization. It encourages individuals to collaborate and form an alliance as a preferred way of collective existence. Islam suggests that it is unnatural that a person can be expected to contain their impulse of discrimination, in favor of their own clan, at the expense of the other. It considers this a human condition that cannot be fully subdued legalistically. This inherent conflict has to be recognized and harmonized through ideas of *ummah*, bound together by faith, and social justice. An Islamic state is pluralistic where people of different culture can live side by side without any fear of discrimination or oppression. A person, as part of a family, tribe or race may have a unique culture but are subservient to the collective good of society which is defined by the universal message. No particular culture is given preference over collective well being when a policy decision is made. Similarly in assigning duties and responsibilities only merit and capability is considered.

In Islam an individual is like a molecule of water that is part of an ocean which may have varying ecological cultures in different parts of the ocean. But each water molecule has to exhibit the same qualities to form an ocean. Extending the same analogy, fish and other species in the ocean are like government functionaries that have to perform their role, but they have to remember that they cannot exist out of water. They are dependent on the water rather than the other way around.

Islam suggests that societies risk their existence when they engage in sinful acts as norms rather than as an exception. A society that loses its moral foundation gets punished in this world for their decadence, as other communities that have stronger character and ethics overtake them. Islam proposes that only individuals will be judged on the Day of Judgment while societies, that are corrupt, will falter through the natural process of evolution.

The Quran emphasizes the importance of learning lessons from past generations and understanding reasons for their demise. It narrates stories of empires that were destroyed when people transgressed the boundaries of ethics. For instance, the stories of Prophet Shuaib (AS) whose people were committing commercial fraud. Or the stories of Prophet Lut (AS), whose people were committing homosexuality. The Quran instructs that although there are rewards for an individual in the afterlife for his good deeds, for societies their condition does not change until the members of a community strive to change it themselves. Through these stories Islam sets up expectations from future societies without engaging in the micro level discussions of outlining the form of government. This lack of mandating a political structure is a blessing considering that the human condition is evolutionary. It defies logic that some Muslim scholars want to imitate the political organization prevalent in the first century of the advent of Islam. A more effective and prudent approach is to develop social structures which are built on values offered by Islam but commensurate with the contemporary social conditions. This approach is in harmony with the concept that human nature has not changed over centuries, but social conditions have evolved with increased knowledge of materials, the universe and the human psyche. Advancement in communication technologies has made it possible for people to interact with each other, which is an important consideration, to develop a social order.

Islamic Social values concentrate on achieving an end which is salvation of the soul without mandating a fixed social structure which could limit the boundaries of human ingenuity to organize their societies. A unique feature of the Islamic Social contract is its evolutionary nature as new interpretations of the Quran emerge using contemporary thought. It is because of this evolutionary condition that social values adopted by a community require review by each new generation. Just like the Quran, Prophet Mohammad (PBUH) did not prescribe a form of government for the *Ummah*. If he had prescribed a particular system, then there would be a group of puritanical Muslims that would refuse to amend it with changing times. We have seen this scenario emerge in other aspects of Muslim lives. In his wisdom, Prophet Mohammad (PBUH) put the onus of responsibility of forming political structures on future leaders to decide. The Charter of Madinah, Treaty of Hudaybiyyah and his sermon during Hajj, few months before his death, provide examples of his prudent approach to politics.

Some theologians propose that for an Islamic Society a constitution is not needed as the Quran offers answers to all questions. This is a misconception as the Quran is neither a book of politics, science nor philosophy. It is a book of Divine wisdom to provide a guideline to mankind in pursuing spiritual, moral and social values. It provides a set of values that can become guiding principles for a society, but it is incumbent upon the community to formulate a constitution that enables them to erect a structure to achieve an equitable, just and free society. As the

The Quran suggests in Verse 13.011 *"Allah does not change a people's lot unless they change what is in their hearts"*. This is exemplified by Prophet Mohammad (PBUH) when he drafted the first known constitution of the Muslim community in the form of Misaq-e-Medinah (See appendix I for complete text of charter of Medinah). From this example of the *Sunnah*, it is evident that each community has to consider its own social, cultural, religious and geographical condition to formulate a constitution that best suits them. This is also evident from the recognition of diverse cultures and races in various Quranic verses.

*(**Verse 22.067**) To every People have We appointed rites and ceremonies which they must follow: let them not then dispute with thee on the matter, but do thou invite (them) to thy Lord: for thou art assuredly on the Right Way.*

*(**Verse 30.022**) And among His Signs is the creation of the heavens and the earth, and the variations in your languages and your colors: verily in that are Signs for those who know.*

(Verse 49.013) *O mankind! We created you from a single (pair) of a male and a female, and made you into nations and tribes, that ye may know each other (not that ye may despise (each other). Verily the most honored of you in the sight of Allah is (he who is) the most righteous of you. And Allah has full knowledge and is well acquainted (with all things).*

Absence of upholding a higher ideal erodes the reason for existence of a society. Islam offers a system in which the Constitution is an operating document while social values are accepted voluntarily by citizens without any force or coercion from the State. Citizenship of an Islamic state is open to all as long as they agree to abide by the values outlined in the constitution. The constitution defines the roles and limitations of executive, legislature and judiciary. It lays down the procedure for election and impeachment of State and elected officials. Islamic Social values, that are humanistic in their intrinsic nature, can be added to the constitution as a minimum condition of citizenship. Any amendment or addition to these social values cannot be decided by an individual, judge or a particular segment of community. Amendments that affect the rights of the citizens are not approved through the agency of parliamentary members but by referring it back to the community by placing it on a ballot paper. This is a truly democratic concept of government by the people for the people, presented by Islam long before its emergence in industrialized world.

In an Islamic system the State has to have minimum influence on the lives of individual citizens. The role of State is limited to ensuring that all citizens have equal rights and live in justice with each other.

Since Islamic social order does not recognize an outside agency, in the form of a corporation or association, is not recognized as a separate entity with its own rights and privileges. Instead, people who manage a corporation are responsible for its performance. A crime committed by a corporation is not the blamed for it but rather on its managers, who are punished if found guilty. A person managing an organization whether commercial, charitable trust or non-profit is considered a custodian during his tenure. In Islamic concept institutionalization is achieved through transfer of trust from a retiring manager to the next one. This is another significant difference from the secular system.

In Islamic view the universe of the believers is one community (*Ummah*) comprising of constellation of nations. It recognizes the emergence of cultures and traditions as well as approves collaboration among diverse people to form a nation state which is managed by local leaders. The State of Medinah was formed through the signing of a constitution among Muslims, Jews and pagans. In this conception a State is a local institution with predefined boundaries to serve community that share cultural or geographic affinity. The State has a responsibility to seek collaboration and cooperation with other Muslim communities, formed in a similar fashion. These two forces, i.e. forming a local community and creating a confederation with other communities, should work together rather than oppose each other. A contemporary example could be the European Union where each independent state is a community with its own unique culture. These communities with geographic affinity have formed a social and economic alliance to safeguard their interests through a confederation.

Social Values

Islam proposes that spirituality of an individual is subjective. A person's approach to God is a personal and private matter. This is probably a key area where secularism agrees with Islamic idea of faith. On the other hand, the social behavior of a person has an effect on other members of the community. A social system has to form a consensus among citizens on collective values to create a community. Secular societies have given the responsibility of developing social values to a democratic system and collective wisdom expressed through majority vote. In this conception, an individual has to accept the values adopted by a society through consent of a majority whether he voluntarily agrees or not. This, in some cases, can create an unbridgeable divergence between personal preferences and collective values adopted by a society at large. Islam promotes faith in one God as a basic human instinct. This position of faith, in a Supreme Creator, is not applied through force rather it is left to the judgment of an individual to voluntarily believe in this abstract idea. A person may use their intellect to justify it through a personal quest. Those that embark on this journey are expected to share their knowledge and experience with others without coercing them to accept it.

Islam presents a set of values derived from revealed Divine wisdom in the Quran and the example of Prophet Mohammad (PBUH). It encourages Muslims to adopt it in their lives because they will be judged on their adherence to it in an afterlife. Collective projection of these individual values becomes the moral character of a just society. Islam proposes that the social system it offers is effective because it is closer to human nature. Do unto others as you would want them to do unto you is the driving principle of all human affairs.

Social values that are presented by Islam are related to temporal matters but have a consequential effect on an individual's spirituality. Upholding justice, managing wealth, paying *zakat* (mandatory charity) and respecting executive authority are social values without any apparent link to faith. It is a person's approach to these values that provides a connection to the salvation of the soul in an afterlife. Islam promotes a hierarchy of loyalties that flows from God then family, neighborhood, State (nation) and *Ummah* (community) in that order. An Islamic State has to be structured so that hierarchy of these loyalties is maintained and harmonized. Islam requires absolute loyalty to God without any hesitation, apprehension or reservation. But this loyalty is voluntary and cannot be forced by an outside agency. Islam guides a person in his natural spheres of influence, as members of family, profession and neighborhood. In terms of order of preference, Islam advises that living a life of social justice has a priority, over performing religious rituals, to attain a higher spiritual rank. As an individual attains higher social stature with greater responsibility; as an elected official, as head of state, or as a judge, he has to comply with an ever-larger sphere of values. Performance of an individual in these community positions will be judged separately, apart from his role as a member of family and neighborhood in the normal course of his life.

All newborn infants are endowed with potentially the same faculties, although their social environments are different. The full potential of these faculties cannot be actualized until it is brought from sub-conscious to conscious through an elaborate system of education. To manifest individual potential, it is expected from a society to provide equitable education opportunity to all its members to be able to have fair chances of success. Focus of the Islamic Social order is to fashion the behavior of an individual to pursue a lifestyle that not only results in a stable community but earns him blessings from the Creator as well. The objective of the Quran is to provide that education and guidance to appreciate the Will of God and exercise it in worldly affairs. Here is one of the examples from the Quran that sets up expectations from a person:

(Verse 31.017) *"O my son! Establish regular prayer, enjoin what is just, and forbid what is wrong: and bear with patient constancy whatever betide thee; for this is firmness (of purpose) in (the conduct of) affairs.* ***(Verse 31.018)*** *"And swell not thy cheek (for pride) at men, nor walk in insolence through the earth; for Allah loveth not any arrogant boaster.* ***(Verse 31.019)*** *"And be moderate in thy pace, and lower thy voice; for the harshest of sounds without doubt is the braying of the ass."*

Islam proposes social values that are mutually inclusive or dependent on each other. It is universally accepted that a person has to be truthful in his dealings with other people. But the same person is advised by Islam to protect defects of others if he happens to know about it. Truthfulness combined with consciousness to respect dignity of fellow citizens is a more positive force than public criticism of others. The idea of ethical behavior in Islam is to create stable social order through exercise of justice, promote mutual respect, and protect individual freedom. It is interesting that most of the social values proposed by the Quran are secular in nature and can be adopted in the form of bill of rights in a constitution, so that they become binding on all members of the community. It is the same practice employed by all constitutional democracies and is in line with the established practices of social organization. Charity is one of the most frequently mentioned social welfare promoted by the Quran. In distributing charity, a person does not have to discriminate based on religion, race or ethnicity. Similarly upholding justice means that a judge will not discriminate based on religion of the parties involved in a court of law. This is the differentiating point between secularist and Islamic social order. Secularism offers values without reference to any divine mandate. Islam on the other hand offers values that are proposed by a Divine Message but are secular in character. Outward practice of upholding these secular values, which are mandated by God, provide an inward spiritual uplift for a practitioner. Secularism recognizes that a society is more paramount than the preferences of an individual. Islam, on the other hand, considers an individual as the key building block that enables emergence of a just society.

In this chapter we present the values that are expected to be upheld by all individual members of a Muslim majority Society.

Nation Building

One of the key components of an Islamic social state is to build a cohesive nation by providing equal rights, maintain unity and appreciate diversity. The following are integral components of nation building.

1- Equal Rights

*(**Verse 6.098**) It is He who hath produced you from a single person: here is a place of sojourn and a place of departure: We detail Our signs for people who understand.*

*(**Verse 10.019**) Mankind was but one nation, but differed (later). Had it not been for a word that went forth before from thy Lord, their differences would have been settled between them.*

*(**Verse 42.008**) If Allah had so willed, He could have made them a single people; but He admits whom He will to His Mercy; and the Wrong-doers will have no protector nor helper.*

Quote from Last sermon of Prophet Mohammad (PBUH):

"All mankind is from Adam and Eve, an Arab has no superiority over a non-Arab nor a non-Arab has any superiority over an Arab; also a white has no superiority over black nor a black has any superiority over white except by piety and good action."

Islam considers that all human beings have equal rights regardless of their ethnic, social and religious background. Social status achieved through education, wealth or position of authority has temporal utility while righteous deeds, during a lifetime, are the differentiating factor in an afterlife. Islamic rituals of communal daily prayers and Hajj, which has to be performed by all Muslims once in a lifetime, promote equality regardless of social status of congregants. God grants all its creatures the designation of a *Khalifa*, vice-regent on earth, without discrimination based on their belief in Him. This equality has to be expressed in granting rights to all citizens to have a voice in the political, social and economic affairs of the community. Prophet

Mohammad (PBUH) was advised by the Quran to consult his companions in political matters of the community. This is a democratic concept in which citizens are required to be active rather than passive. In a way, in worldly affairs the Prophet was dependent on his companions even though his decisions, once announced, were final and binding on all of them.

It is important to note that social equality is based on the concept that the differentiating factor in society is contributions to the community rather than parochial factors i.e. ethnicity or wealth. The Quran makes it quite clear that people are ranked based on their deeds rather than their heritage, wealth or social status. In his last Hajj sermon Prophet Mohammad (PBUH) declared that there should be no difference between an Arab and non-Arab in his *Ummah* (community). In an Islamic concept equality of rights does not mean that there are no income inequalities or that it approves socialism. Islam recognizes that there are variations in capabilities and talents; function of the State is to provide equal opportunity to all its citizens in their endeavors. The State does not have the right to reduce income inequality through exercise of its coercive power. It is expected that citizens will voluntarily share their good fortune with others by sponsoring charitable endowments and offering help to those that are downtrodden. To induce this attitude of giving, the State can offer incentives, but the real motivation should be to receive the blessings of God. It is also expected from the individual that they will not use their financial muscle and wealth to gain unlawful advantage over others or break the law without impunity. In return for this charity God promises that they will experience expansion in their prosperity as well as get a reward in afterlife.

2- Maintain Unity

(Verse 3.103) *And hold fast, all together, by the rope which Allah (stretches out for you), and be not divided among yourselves; and remember with gratitude Allah's favour on you; for ye were enemies and He joined your hearts in love, so that by His Grace, ye became brethren; and ye were on the brink of the pit of Fire, and He saved you from it. Thus doth Allah make His Signs clear to you: That ye may be* *guided.*

(Verse 6.038) *There is not an animal (that lives) on the earth, nor a being that flies on its wings, but (forms part of) communities like you. Nothing have we omitted from the Book, and they (all) shall be gathered to their Lord in the end.*

(Verse 6.159) *As for those who divide their religion and break up into sects, thou hast no part in them in the least: their affair is with Allah: He will in the end tell them the truth of all that they did.*

(Verse 16.092) *And be not like a woman who breaks into untwisted strands the yarn which she has spun, after it has become strong. Nor take your oaths to practice deception between yourselves, lest one party should be more numerous than another: for Allah will test you by this; and on the Day of Judgment He will certainly make clear to you (the truth of) that wherein ye disagree.*

(Verse 21.092) *Verily, this brotherhood of yours is a single brotherhood, and I am your Lord and Cherisher: therefore serve Me (and no other).*

(Verse 23.052) *And verily this Brotherhood of yours is a single Brotherhood, and I am your Lord and Cherisher: therefore fear Me (and no other).* ***(Verse 23.053)*** *But people have cut off their affair (of unity), between them, into sects: each party rejoices in that which is with itself.*

(Verse 30.032) *Those who split up their Religion, and become (mere) Sects,- each party rejoicing in that which is with itself!*

(Verse 49.009) *If two parties among the Believers fall into a quarrel, make ye peace between them: but if one of them transgresses beyond bounds against the other, then fight ye (all) against the one that transgresses until it complies with the command of Allah; but if it complies, then make peace between them with justice, and be fair: for Allah loves those who are fair (and just).*

We can draw following conclusions from the preceding verses:

1. Mankind may have apparent differences in culture and traditions, but they form a single humanity. Human nature is universal.
2. It is always harder to maintain unity than creating divisions. Primary objective of an Islamic Social state is to ensure unity among people through exercise of social justice.
3. It is expected that citizens of the State will stand with those who

are oppressed so that justice prevails, which is the only sure way of maintaining unity.

Islam informs its adherents to prevent dividing a community into sects. That does not mean Islam does not recognize diversity of cultures, doctrines and faiths.

It shows that diversity is part of Divine design. Islamic social state should not differentiate between people based on their ethnic and cultural background but rather deal with them justly. State positions and functions should not be distributed based on cultural affiliations but rather on merit and individual capability.

3- Appreciate diversity

(Verse 2.148) *To each is a goal to which Allah turns him; then strive together (as in a race) Towards all that is good. Wheresoever ye are, Allah will bring you Together. For Allah Hath power over all things.* ***(Verse 2.149)*** *From whencesoever Thou startest forth, turn Thy face in the direction of the sacred Mosque; that is indeed the truth from the Lord. And Allah is not unmindful of what ye do.*

(Verse 11.118) *If thy Lord had so willed, He could have made mankind one people: but they will not cease to dispute.*

(Verse 16.093) *If Allah so willed, He could make you all one people: But He leaves straying whom He pleases, and He guides whom He pleases: but ye shall certainly be called to account for all your actions.*

(Verse 22.067) *To every People have We appointed rites and ceremonies which they must follow: let them not then dispute with thee on the matter, but do thou invite (them) to thy Lord: for thou art assuredly on the Right Way.*

(Verse 30.022) *And among His Signs is the creation of the heavens and the earth, and the variations in your languages and your colors: verily in that are Signs for those who know.*

(Verse 49.013) *O mankind! We created you from a single (pair) of a male and a female, and made you into nations and tribes, that ye may know each other (not that ye may despise (each other). Verily the most honored of you in the sight of*

Allah is (he who is) the most righteous of you. And Allah has full knowledge and is well acquainted (with all things).

There is no nation in the world which can claim to be 100% homogeneous without the presence of any other ethnic or religious group. Turkey has majority of Turkic speaking people, but it also has a presence of Kurds and Uzbeks. Similarly, it is a majority Muslim country, but it has a presence of Jewish and Christian communities as well. Pakistan, a majority Muslim country, has Christian and Hindu populations as well as ethnic diversity represented by Sindhi, Saraiki, Punjabi, Pashton, Baloch and Urdu speaking communities. Algeria has Berber and Arabic speaking communities. It is the same situation in all other countries around the world.

The ideal of a socially just society mandated by the Quran cannot exist unless it fully recognizes the diversity of cultures and faiths. Islam recognizes that mankind has evolved into many different races with their own unique culture and tradition. Islam, appreciating this diversity, allows freedom to people to practice rites as indicated in verse 22.067. In the Islamic concept a State is an administrative unit that may evolve its own unique culture over a period of time but the ultimate allegiance of the people of State is to one God and His Prophet. The State has to ensure that all ethnicities are fairly treated in terms of allocation of resources and sharing of bounties. This is especially important for Muslim majority states with ethnic diversity for instance Malaysia and Pakistan. Legislation that restricts cultural expression or creates provinces on a particular ethnicity is against values of a social state proposed by Islam. People are judged based on their good deeds and contribution towards society rather than their ethnicity or membership in a religious sect as indicated in verse 49.013.

Upholding Justice

No secular society can guarantee that they can impart justice without fail. This failure of temporal society, to ensure justice, could become a source of despair especially among the poor and downtrodden. The Divine law of equality proposes that all humans have equal rights and will have recourse to get recompense for an injustice that was unnoticed by a worldly system. Faith in a Supreme Arbiter of justice provides a sense of hope without which it would be impossible to maintain sanity and function properly.

Islam advises people that their intentions may not be visible to others but does not escape the Divine justice. The Quran informs us that God knows what is hidden in the thought of the person and he will be accounted for it in the afterlife. It also advises that judging intentions are a domain of God alone and people should respect outwardly expressed good intention of a person without doubt. To impart absolute justice requires the existence of an arbiter that does not fail to record events as a witness. The Quran speaks about God's ability to know in following terms:

*(**Verse 11.123**) To Allah do belong the unseen (secrets) of the heavens and the earth, and to Him goeth back every affair (for decision): then worship Him, and put thy trust in Him: and thy Lord is not unmindful of aught that ye do.*

*(**Verse 13.009**) He knoweth the unseen and that which is open: He is the Great, the Most High.*

*(**Verse 14.038**) "O our Lord! Truly Thou dost know what we conceal and what we reveal: for nothing is hidden from Allah, whether on earth or in heaven."*

*(**Verse 17.036**) And pursue not that of which thou hast no knowledge; for every act of hearing, or of seeing or of (feeling in) the heart will be enquired into (on the Day of Reckoning).*

*(**Verse 21.004**) Say: "My Lord knoweth (every) word (spoken) in the heavens and on earth: He is the One that heareth and knoweth (all things)."*

*(**Verse 21.110**) "It is He Who knows what is open in speech and what ye hide (in your hearts).*

*(**Verse 27.065**) Say: None in the heavens or on earth, except Allah, knows what is hidden: nor can they perceive when they shall be raised up (for Judgment).*

*(**Verse 58.007**) Seest thou not that Allah doth know (all) that is in the heavens and on earth? There is not a secret consultation between three, but He makes the fourth among them, - Nor between five but He makes the sixth,- nor between fewer nor more, but He is in their midst, wheresoever they be: In the end will He tell them the truth of their conduct, on the Day of Judgment. For Allah has full knowledge of all things.*

According to Islam injustices are of two types. A person may commit an injustice to himself, or he may cause injury to another person by his actions. Personal injustice is related to overstepping the boundaries recommended by Islam for righteous behavior. This injures the soul which will be subjected to Divine Justice on the Day of Judgment. These intangible injustices cannot be tried in a court of law as there is no temporal manifestation. An example could be personal faith where a person rejects Oneness of God. This is an injustice that does not hurt anyone else but the person himself as he will be questioned about it on the Day of Judgment.

(Verse 6.151) *Say: "Come, I will rehearse what Allah hath (really) prohibited you from": Join not anything as equal with Him; be good to your parents; kill not your children on a plea of want;- We provide sustenance for you and for them;- come not nigh to shameful deeds. Whether open or secret; take not life, which Allah hath made sacred, except by way of justice and law: thus doth He command you, that ye may learn wisdom.*

Verse 6.151 offers a good example of injustices done to oneself which are bad behavior with children or committing shameful deeds whether they are open or secret. Mistreatment of parents or joining others with God, these may not be punishable by a court of law but are injustices to which a person will be held accountable in afterlife.

The Quran instructs that humans were created as social species requiring help from others to realize their potential.

(Verse 6.038) *There is not an animal (that lives) on the earth, nor a being that flies on its wings, but (forms part of) communities like you. Nothing have we omitted from the Book, and they (all) shall be gathered to their Lord in the end.*

Upholding justice is an important glue to creating communal bonds. Islam promotes an idea of justice where a person has to realize that to achieve his own potential, he has to practice justice towards himself as well as others. From this perspective setting up moral police by some conservative Muslim majority societies does not meet the criteria of justice laid down in many verses of the Quran. The Quran instructs that it is possible that a person can be acquitted by a worldly court for crimes committed because of lack of evidence but there is no avoidance of penalty in the afterlife. Islam prefers a personal self-restraint when it comes to leading a just life.

There are many instances when a person may be doing an outward good, but the intentions could be safeguarding a worldly self-interest. For instance, a corporation or an individual may be giving to charity to help a cause but they may be gaining a tax advantage that is higher than the amount donated. The net effect is that the donor is a net gainer in the world rather than being altruistic by seeking a reward in the afterlife. In reality the community is a net loser although a segment of society might have benefited from it, which includes the charity organization and the donors. In the Islamic concept of justice this kind of behavior is looked down upon. It is expected that all citizens will discharge their fiduciary communal responsibility in a way that their intention of doing good should be reflected in ascertaining that there is a net gain rather than a loss to the community.

Quran instructs people to ensure justice in the following verses:

(Verse 2.042) *And cover not Truth with falsehood, nor conceal the Truth when ye know (what it is).*

(Verse 6.115) *The word of thy Lord doth find its fulfillment in truth and in justice: None can change His words: for He is the one who heareth and knoweth all.*

(Verse 5.008) *O ye who believe! stand out firmly for Allah, as witnesses to fair dealing, and let not the hatred of others to you make you swerve to wrong and depart from justice. Be just: that is next to piety: and fear Allah. For Allah is well-acquainted with all that ye do.*

(Verse 8.029) *O ye who believe! if ye fear Allah, He will grant you a criterion (to judge between right and wrong), remove from you (all) evil (that may afflict) you, and forgive you: for Allah is the Lord of grace unbounded.*

(Verse 45.022) *Allah created the heavens and the earth for just ends, and in order that each soul may find the recompense of what it has earned, and none of them be wronged.*

(Verse 46.019) *And to all are (assigned) degrees according to the deeds which they (have done), and in order that (Allah) may recompense their deeds, and no injustice be done to them.*

The Quran advises believers to speak the truth about their intentions in their mutual affairs. Only then is justice established in the world and blessings earned in the afterlife. Justice can only be imparted when the intent of the person is ascertained in prosecuting a crime. For instance, when someone is killed one of the first thing to ascertain is whether the murder was pre-meditated or occurred by error or in the heat of a moment. The penalty for both is different. Pre-meditated murder gets a severe punishment when proven in a court of law. But it is very hard to determine if a murder was pre-meditated in cases where the convict pleads not guilty. Only the outward actions of a person i.e. the word spoken by the convict to people before and after the murder; witnesses to the scene and the tool of murder can shed light if the murder was pre-meditated. In terms of collection of evidence, it is important to note that the means of collection of evidence should be lawful. For example, State officials cannot enter a house without proper authorization to search and collect evidence. Similarly, witnesses cannot be forced to provide evidence.

The system of justice employed by a State cannot function effectively unless each member discharges their responsibility to uphold justice. It is expected that citizens will not hesitate to come forward to give evidence against a crime they have witnessed and that they will be truthful and without bias. Similarly, the judge is expected to be fair and without coercive pressure from an external agency. Judges have to remember that the objective of a justice system is to reform the convict and award fair compensation to the effected party for damage done to them.

In the Islamic system of justice, a person that wrongly accuses another person is punishable as well.

*(**Verse 24.004**) And those who launch a charge against chaste women, and produce not four witnesses (to support their allegations),- flog them with eighty stripes; and reject their evidence ever after: for such men are wicked transgressors;-*

From the above verse it is evident if someone engages in false accusations then they are not only punished for it but also barred from ever providing evidence in a court of law.

It is wrongly believed that the concept of justice only applies to the criminal justice system. Islam instructs believers to adopt a lifestyle of justice that is discernible in all their actions. It is expected that a person will employ justice in discharging their professional responsibilities; in dealing with family members; in commercial transactions; as member of a community and in their approach to God.

Justice towards God requires efforts to understand tenets of the religion and creating a balance between prayer and social responsibilities. The Islamic value of justice is all encompassing.

Freedom of Religion

*(**Verse 2.256**) Let there be no compulsion in religion: Truth stands out clear from Error: whoever rejects evil and believes in Allah hath grasped the most trustworthy hand-hold, that never breaks. And Allah heareth and knoweth all things.*

*(**Verse 2.272**) It is not required of thee (O Messenger), to set them on the right path, but Allah sets on the right path whom He pleaseth. Whatever of good ye give benefits your own souls, and ye shall only do so seeking the "Face" of Allah. Whatever good ye give, shall be rendered back to you, and ye shall not Be dealt with unjustly.*

*(**Verse 6.107**) If it had been Allah's plan, they would not have taken false gods: but We made thee not one to watch over their doings, nor art thou set over them to dispose of their affairs.*

*(**Verse 6.108**) Revile not ye those whom they call upon besides Allah, lest they out of spite revile Allah in their ignorance. Thus have We made alluring to each people its own doings. In the end will they return to their Lord, and We shall then tell them the truth of all that they did.*

*(**Verse 6.149**) Say: "With Allah is the argument that reaches home: if it had been His will, He could indeed have guided you all."*

*(**Verse 10.011**) If Allah were to hasten for men the ill (they have earned) as they would fain hasten on the good,- then would their respite be settled at once. But We leave those who rest not their hope on their meeting with Us, in their trespasses, wandering in distraction to and fro.*

*(**Verse 10.099**) If it had been thy Lord's will, they would all have believed,- all who are on earth! wilt thou then compel mankind, against their will, to believe!*

(Verse 10.100) *No soul can believe, except by the will of Allah, and He will place doubt (or obscurity) on those who will not understand.*

(Verse 11.008) *If We delay the penalty for them for a definite term, they are sure to say, "What keeps it back?" Ah! On the day it (actually) reaches them, nothing will turn it away from them, and they will be completely encircled by that which they used to mock at!* ***(Verse 11.009)*** *If We give man a taste of Mercy from Ourselves, and then withdraw it from him, behold! he is in despair and (falls into) blasphemy.*

(Verse 15.003) *Leave them alone, to enjoy (the good things of this life) and to please themselves: let (false) hope amuse them: soon will knowledge (undeceive them).* ***(Verse 15.004)*** *Never did We destroy a population that had not a term decreed and assigned beforehand.*

(Verse 16.061) *If Allah were to punish men for their wrong-doing, He would not leave, on the (earth), a single living creature: but He gives them respite for a stated Term: When their Term expires, they would not be able to delay (the punishment) for a single hour, just as they would not be able to anticipate it (for a single hour).*

(Verse 18.029) *Say, "The truth is from your Lord": Let him who will believe, and let him who will, reject (it): for the wrong-doers We have prepared a Fire whose (smoke and flames), like the walls and roof of a tent, will hem them in: if they implore relief they will be granted water like melted brass, that will scald their faces, how dreadful the drink! How uncomfortable a couch to recline on!*

(Verse 18.058) *But your Lord is Most forgiving, full of Mercy. If He were to call them (at once) to account for what they have earned, then surely He would have hastened their punishment:*

but they have their appointed time, beyond which they will find no refuge.

(Verse 26.003) *It may be thou frettest thy soul with grief, that they do not become Believers.* ***(Verse 26.004)*** *If (such) were Our Will, We could send down to them from the sky a Sign, to which they would bend their necks in humility.*

(Verse 35.045) *If Allah were to punish men according to what they deserve. He would not leave on the back of the (earth) a single living creature: but He gives them respite for a stated Term: when their Term expires, verily Allah has in His sight all His Servants.*

(Verse 45.014) *Tell those who believe, to forgive those who do not look forward to the Days of Allah: It is for Him to recompense (for good or ill) each People according* *to what they have earned.*

Preceding Quranic verses are just few of many more that demonstrates complete freedom of religion in an Islamic social order. There are a few important concepts to note from these verses:

1. If it was the Divine Will then all mankind would follow one religion. It is by God's leave that people have the freedom to choose their faith. Finding true faith is a challenge for which guidance is provided through revealed books and Prophets. It cannot be a function of State to interfere in matters of faith as this is strictly domain of God.
2. Even Prophet Mohammad (PBUH) (verse 2.272 & 26.003) did not have the right to force people to accept the message of Islam. His role was to inform people through revealed words and provide an example from his life. It was left to the people to accept this faith through the exercise of their free will.
3. Judging people about the truthfulness of their faith is the domain of God (verse 15.003, 18.058, 35.045, & 45.014). No human agency, including the State, has the right to judge, persecute and discriminate among people, based on their religious beliefs.
4. God does not discriminate in blessing people with his bounties based on their faith in Him (verse 16.061). This implies that no temporal authority can claim to have the right to discriminate among people that form a community.
5. A person has complete independence in choosing a faith (verse 2.256)
6. It is expected that Muslims will respect the faith of others so that others respect their faith (verse 6.108)

Islam offers complete freedom of religion to all humans. No entity is allowed to coerce people to accept a particular faith. Muslims can preach their religion peacefully, but it is preferred that they convert others by the demonstrated excellence of their character in daily life. That is the reason Prophet Mohammad (PBUH) demonstrated a good example of character before he started preaching his message of Islam. He was given titles of *Sadiq* (truthful) and *Ameen* (trustworthy) by Meccan community because of his conduct.

The Islamic State is required to provide protection and guarantee freedom of religion to all its citizens including non-Muslims. Since non-Muslims are not required to pay *Zakat*, a religiously mandated charity, they pay a tax called *Jizya* for the protection and social services provided by the State. *Jizya* is more an equalizer rather than a source of discrimination against non-Muslims. Sociologically absence of *Jizya* could be tantamount to excluding non-Muslims to play their communal role as full citizens. The concept of no-representation without taxation was first presented by Islam in its introduction of *jizya* for non-Muslims and *Zakat* for Muslim citizens. Throughout Islamic history, starting from *Rashidun* (rightly guided) Caliphs until the Ottoman Empire, non-Muslims were given important positions in government. Distrust of non-Muslims, to assume position of authority, is a recent phenomenon resulting from memories of discrimination during the colonial rule of Christian Imperial powers. Fears of proxy re-conquest produce attitudes that are wrongly associated with the social message of Islam.

In the 21st century societies are managed through rules outlined in a constitution and political power that is derived from a majority mandate through popular vote. Islamic concept of a social state does not bar non-Muslims from assuming any role, including the head of government, if they agree to abide by the values laid down in the constitution. This right is granted to them by God with deferment of judgment of beliefs until the afterlife. God also does not discriminate in granting the privileged status of a vice regency to all men. As an operating document, the constitution should not bar any citizen, because of their religious beliefs, from contesting elections for the highest office. Election of a non-Muslim head of government does not equate to acceptance of un-Islamic values because he is only an operative head while legislative powers are vested in the *Majlis-e-Shura* (parliament) and citizens at large. Secondly, for heads of government to maintain political power they have to respect the views and opinions of the majority of people. Thirdly political power is not concentrated in the office of head of government alone. He has to rely on his cabinet members that are mostly from the majority Muslim population. A non-Muslim head of government that tries to favor his own coreligionist will lose his mandate awarded by an Islamic Social justice system that promotes equity and merit. Realistically it is unlikely that majorities in Islamic or secular constituents will elect someone that is not an adherent of a majority faith. Even in secular democracies it is highly unlikely that a Muslim candidate can be elected as the head of government in Christian dominated Western democracies. This fact was made evident during the election of American President Barack Hussein Obama when he had to go out of his way to prove his adherence to the Christian faith.

The Islamic concept of freedom of religion is not just related to non-Muslims but include Muslims as well. It is incumbent upon the State to ensure religion is not suppressed and people are free to practice their religious duties and obligations. If a State prevents people from performing their religious rites, then it is justified for people to protest and overthrow that government. In Islam religious practices are divided into spiritual and social. Spiritual rites like five daily prayers, the month of fasting and *Hajj* are voluntary in nature. Islam considers spirituality of a person to be a private matter and judged differently from communal rights of the people on each other. It is for this reason, when Prophet Mohammad (PBUH) declared his message, for the first time, he asked people whether they considered him a truthful, trustworthy and honest person which are social values. He took evidence from them about his social behavior rather than his personal conviction about oneness of God which was a private matter hidden from the eyes of the people. There is only one mandatory religious duty for Muslims which is paying *zakat,* and every eligible person has to pay it without relief. The State can intervene to deduct *zakat* from those who try to abstain from it. It is interesting that mandatory condition is for a religious duty that is an instrument of social justice. It benefits society rather than any individual.

Islam promotes establishment of a faith-based society which requires inclusion of religion as part of the school curriculum. Courses on all religions have to be made available in schools although enrollment of students should be optional rather than mandatory. It is the State's responsibility to make the resources available for religious education, but it is the right of parents as guardians to decide about enrolling their children for religious courses.

In many Muslim countries State issued identification documents include information about religion. Many secularists argue that this is discriminatory, as religion is a private matter which need not be disclosed publicly. In that sense identification of people through race, gender, age and family surname should also be considered discriminatory. It is true that in Muslim countries incidents of discrimination against non-Muslims are more prevalent. The choice of including information of religion should be a decision of the community at large. But if it is adopted then society must ensure protection against discrimination and persecution. In some extreme cases religious identity can cause social reprisal which is aggravated in the absence of an expedient judicial system. Recent division of Sudan, into two sovereign entities, was purely on religious grounds. In an Islamic social state, built on the message of Quran and *Sunnah*, a person's identification through faith is not a source of discrimination but rather to respect their religious traditions in their professional and communal life. This fact is evident from the instructions Hazrat Ali (RATA), fourth among the *Rashidun* (rightly guided) caliphs, gave to his governor of Egypt where the majority were Christians:

"Infuse your heart with mercy, love and kindness for your subjects. Be not in face of them a voracious animal, counting them as easy prey, for they are of two kinds: ***either they are your brothers in religion or your equals in creation.*** *Error catches them unaware, deficiencies overcome them, [evil deeds] are committed by them intentionally and by mistake. So grant them your pardon and your forgiveness to the same extent that you hope God will grant you His pardon and forgiveness. For you are above them, and he who appointed you is above you, and God is above him who appointed you."*

(Source: Islamic Democratic Discourse by M.A. Muqtedar, page 188)

This instruction was a worldly manifestation of the verse from Quran:

(Verse 5.048) *To thee We sent the Scripture in truth, confirming the scripture that came before it, and guarding it in safety: so judge between them by what Allah* *hath revealed, and follow not their vain desires, diverging from the Truth that hath come to thee. To each among you have we prescribed a law and an open way. If Allah had so willed, He would have made you a single people, but (His plan is) to test you in what He hath given you:* ***so strive as in a race in all virtues****. The goal of you all is to Allah; it is He that will show you the truth of the matters in which ye dispute;*

Freedom of Expression

(Verse 4.148) *Allah loveth not that evil should be noised abroad in public speech, except where injustice hath been done; for Allah is He who heareth and knoweth all things.* ***(Verse 4.149)*** *Whether ye publish a good deed or conceal it or cover evil with pardon, verily Allah doth blot out (sins) and hath power (in the judgment of values).*

(Verse 6.108) *Revile not ye those whom they call upon besides Allah, lest they out of spite revile Allah in their ignorance. Thus have We made alluring to each people its own doings. In the end will they return to their Lord, and We shall then tell them the truth of all that they did.*

(Verse 7.146) *Those who behave arrogantly on the earth in defiance of right - them will I turn away from My signs: Even if they see all the signs, they will not believe in them; and if they see the way of right conduct, they will not adopt it as the way; but if they see the way of error, that is the way they will adopt. For they have rejected our signs, and failed to take warning from them.*

(Verse 17.053) *Say to My servants that they should (only) say those things that are best: for Satan doth sow dissensions among them: For Satan is to man an avowed enemy.*

(Verse 24.030) *Say to the believing men that they should lower their gaze and guard their modesty: that will make for greater purity for them: And Allah is well acquainted with all that they do.*

(Verse 25.063) *And the servants of (Allah) Most Gracious are those who walk on the earth in humility, and when the ignorant address them, they say, "Peace!";*

(Verse 22.067) *To every People have We appointed rites and ceremonies which they must follow: let them not then dispute with thee on the matter, but do thou* *invite (them) to thy Lord: for thou art assuredly on the Right Way.*

(Verse 49.011) *O ye who believe! Let not some men among you laugh at others: It may be that the (latter) are better than the (former): Nor let some women laugh at others: It may be that the (latter are better than the (former): Nor defame nor be sarcastic to each other, nor call each other by (offensive) nicknames: Ill-seeming is a name connoting wickedness, (to be used of one) after he has believed: And those who do not desist are (indeed) doing wrong.*

Islam offers equal right of expression to speak the truth and be able to protest injustices. Preceding verses of the Quran makes it clear that freedom of expression offers people an opportunity to promote good values. The following sums up the Islamic concept of freedom of expression:

1. People should not use liberty of expression to create dissent, unrest and anarchy in society. Rather they should raise their voice to uphold justice.
2. Using expression of wealth and stature to influence law or gain concessions from government functionaries is looked down upon by Islam.
3. Public expression should not be used to laugh at a segment of a society or an individual. For instance, publication of cartoons to defame Prophet Jesus (AS) cannot be allowed in an Islamic state as it is disrespectful to a Prophet as well as to a large segment of humanity that follow his message. This does not mean that historians and scholars cannot write analysis and commentaries.

The Islamic State offers complete freedom of expression to all its citizens, but this liberty should not be abused to create public unrest, create divisions or do mischief in the society. Hate speech and defamation is looked upon by Islam (verse 6.108). Sadly, many Muslim scholars in their Friday sermons spread ideas of hate against other sects or religions. Similarly, politicians in many Muslim countries use their political platforms to create ethnic divisions. These expressions are an abuse of the right and strongly condemned by many verses in the Quran (for example verse 4.148).

The Quran enjoins it on all Muslims to raise their voice against injustice. But there is one important qualification here. A citizen that notices an abuse of authority or corruption of a state functionary should bring it to the notice of the proper authorities instead of creating public unrest by resorting to violent protests. If the issue is not resolved, then the person is required to create public awareness to apprehend the dishonest functionary. A person has the liberty to criticize policies of the government or present their views on policies. In modern democracies the media and civic organizations play this role. The State as well as the community has to ensure that whistle blowers are protected from persecution by standing up with them.

Publishing derogatory speech about another faith is an un-Islamic practice and cannot be allowed in an Islamic Social State. Spreading rumors or defamatory information without ascertaining facts is considered a serious breach of mutual respect and trust between citizens. In a similar manner being sarcastic or name calling is considered detrimental to maintaining cohesiveness and unity.

Women's Rights

(Verse 2.241) *For divorced women maintenance (should be provided) on a reasonable (scale). This is a duty on the righteous.*

(Verse 4.001) *O mankind! reverence your Guardian-Lord, who created you from a single person, created, of like nature, His mate, and from them twain scattered (like seeds) countless men and women;- reverence Allah, through whom ye demand your mutual (rights), and (reverence) the wombs (That bore you): for Allah ever watches over you.*

(Verse 4.019) *O ye who believe! Ye are forbidden to inherit women against their will. Nor should ye treat them with harshness, that ye may take away part of the dower ye have given them, except where they have been guilty of open lewdness; on the contrary live with them on a footing of kindness and equity. If ye take a dislike to them it may be that ye dislike a thing, and Allah brings about through it a great deal of good.*

(Verse 4.128) *If a wife fears cruelty or desertion on her husband's part, there is* *no blame on them if they arrange an amicable settlement between themselves; and such settlement is best; even though men's souls are swayed by greed. But if ye do good and practice self-restraint, Allah is well-acquainted with all that ye do.*

*(**Verse 4.034**) Men are the protectors and maintainers of women, because Allah has given the one more (strength) than the other, and because they support them from their means. Therefore the righteous women are devoutly obedient, and guard in (the husband's) absence what Allah would have them guard. As to those women on whose part ye fear disloyalty and ill-conduct, admonish them (first), (Next), refuse to share their beds, (And last) beat them (lightly); but if they return to obedience, seek not against them Means (of annoyance): For Allah is Most High, great (above you all).*

*(**Verse 7.189**) It is He Who created you from a single person, and made his mate of like nature, in order that he might dwell with her (in love). When they are united, she bears a light burden and carries it about (unnoticed). When she grows heavy, they both pray to Allah their Lord, (saying): "If Thou givest us a goodly child, we vow we shall (ever) be grateful."*

*(**Verse 24.004**) And those who launch a charge against chaste women, and produce not four witnesses (to support their allegations),- flog them with eighty stripes; and reject their evidence ever after: for such men are wicked transgressors;-*

*(**Verse 24.023**) Those who slander chaste women, indiscreet but believing, are cursed in this life and in the Hereafter: for them is a grievous Penalty,- (**Verse 24.024**) On the Day when their tongues, their hands, and their feet will bear witness against them as to their actions.*

*(**Verse 30.021**) And among His Signs is this, that He created for you mates from among yourselves, that ye may dwell in tranquility with them, and He has put love and mercy between your (hearts): verily in that are Signs for those who reflect.*

*(**Verse 58.001**) Allah has indeed heard (and accepted) the statement of the woman who pleads with thee concerning her husband and carries her complaint (in prayer) to Allah: and Allah (always) hears the arguments between both sides among you: for Allah hears and sees (all things).*

*(**Verse 53.045**) That He did create in pairs,- male and female,*

*(**Verse 75.039**) And of him He made two sexes, male and female.*

Quote from Last Hajj sermon of Prophet Mohammad (PBUH):

"O People, it is true that you have certain rights with regard to your women, but they also have rights over you. Remember that you have taken them as your wives only under Allah's trust and with His permission. If they abide by your right then to them belongs the right to be fed and clothed in kindness. Do treat your women well and be kind to them for they are your partners and committed helpers. And it is your right that they do not make friends with any one of whom you do not approve, as well as never to be unchaste."

Unlike other religions Islam offers women equal social standing with men. When the Quran speaks to believers it does not speak to men alone but both genders. There is an incorrect mythical story prevalent in Muslim societies that women were created from the rib of Adam symbolically subjugating them to male dominance. This story is not validated by the Quran rather it is widely believed to be emanating from Christian tradition. In verses that relates to the story of Adam and subsequent development of communities, God instructs that He created mates each with their own responsibility. The Quran narrates stories of many women that played a significant role in supporting Prophets in the promotion of their message. There is the story of Sarah wife of Abraham and mother of Ishaq; Hagar wife of Abraham and mother of Ishmael; Mary mother of Hazrat Issa (Jesus); Sheba Queen of current day Ethiopia during the time of Prophet Solomon (AS); Khadija wife of Prophet Mohammad (PBUH); and Fatima, daughter of the Prophet, wife of Ali and mother of Hassan and Hussain. All these women played significant roles in the establishment of religion that was promoted by the Prophets and their companions. In a way they depended on their women to gain strength when the tide of public opinion was rising against them.

It is significant that the Quran, a Divine Revelation, does not talk about rights of men as a gender but it does protect the rights of women mandated by God. Islam sanctified the rights of women by presenting the pre-nuptial conditions of marriage and divorce; granted them a share in inheritance as sisters, daughters, mothers and wife; granted rights to mothers during their pregnancy, nursing of infants and in old age; and respected the right of widows to remarry. This was unusual for its time. In contemporary times women in Islamic countries are restricted in terms of access to higher education, consent to marriage or persuasion of a profession. All these limits are un-Islamic and must be repealed. In an Islamic Social State women play a significant role not only in terms of social development but also in economic prosperity of the society. Hazarat Khadija (RATA) was a businesswoman and employed Prophet Mohammad (PBUH) as her agent. Prophet Mohammad (PBUH) respected and valued her so much that he did not marry anyone else while Hazrat Khadija (RATA), a widow who was fifteen years his senior, was alive. Similarly, his other wife Aisha (RATA) was actively engaged in the political affairs of the community after the death of Prophet Mohammad (PBUH) and provided guidance on many occasions. She is one of the most quoted sources of *hadith*. Muslim societies should learn from these examples and understand the rightful role of women in their societies.

Women would have to try to fully appreciate the Islamic tenets related to their roles as mothers, sisters, daughters, professionals and wives. From the Quranic verses the prime responsibility of women is building characters of their children and ensuring that the men in their lives lead a morally ethical life. The contribution of mothers is critical especially for nurturing children under the age of five. It is now established by behavioral psychiatrists that children acquire their basic character within the first five years that dominate their attitude throughout their lives. It is also established that an infant is most vulnerable to physical as well as psychological traumas. Although fathers have to play a role, it is the mother that has a special bond with her child that is critical in attending to the seed that grows to become a secure and durable human being. In an Islamic State, mothers that are fostering small children should be given special privileges in terms of healthcare, access to parenting guidance as well as flexible work hours and reduced workload.

Psychologists have learned that a stable family requires the presence of a mother and a father. It is for this reason Islam looks down upon divorce and advises Muslims to be mindful in matters related to the health of families. In modern societies both men and women earn an income. It is wrongly assumed in Muslim communities that provision of livelihood is the prime responsibility of men while mending home is primarily domain of women. If we look at the life of Prophet Mohammad (PBUH), Hazrat Khadija (RATA) was the business owner while the Prophet was her agent. In other words, she provided him an employment. The important thing to remember here is that Islam elaborates the division of labor in a family. The role of men is still predominantly related to safety and protection of family unit while women's role is nurturing, nutritional and character builder. In these roles men can facilitate women but are hardly effective as a leader. Men are just not capable of making a home, alone, even if they try their best to do that. Demands of building and retaining families are one of the top responsibilities of women that they have to balance with a profession. Being a mother or wife does not mean that a woman should be barred from pursuing a professional career. Women must realize that they have to prioritize their life based on the family responsibilities that they have. Islam prefers that women give preference to taking care of infant children and reduce their professional commitments during those formative years. Local social security organizations and State have to provide financial support to families that are dependent on two incomes during the last trimester of pregnancy and first few years of tending infant children.

Women have to play a significant role in economic and social development of their societies Islam does not restrict women from pursuing any profession, but it does emphasize that the female gender is stronger in intellect while at the same time relatively weaker in muscle power. Muscular weakness is evident from the physiology of male and female bodies. It is more a function of hormones and nature than discrimination. Women's bodies are more complex as compared to men because of the special functions needed to carry a fetus for nine months during pregnancy. Women engaged in blue collar professions, that require strength of muscles, have a higher probability of internal injuries and hormonal imbalances. This means that some professions where a person uses intelligence rather than muscle are more suitable for women like tailoring, beauticians, accountants, software developers, doctors, teachers, lawyers, manager, product assembly, confectionery, business ownership, call center operators and many more. In rural areas women play a significant role in horticulture and animal husbandry services. Working as a construction worker or a warehouse operator may not be suitable for women just because of their physiology. In Western countries, where recognition of gender difference has been disappearing, women engaged in male dominated industries for instance truck driving, construction work and warehousing, have expressed difficulties faced by them in pursuing these careers at the cost of their family lives as well as complexities in rearing children. This does not mean that any profession can be out of reach of women. During Muslim conquest of Syria and Iraq in 1st century after *Hijrah* (migration), women were part of armies not only as nurses and cook but also as soldiers working as rear guard. Second Caliph Umar appointed a woman as an inspector of the markets. In general, a profession where a person has to utilize brain than muscle is more suitable for women according to Islamic presentation of difference in gender.

Some feminists raise the issue that Islam allows men polygamy while women have to remain monogamous. The concept of polygamy is widely abused by Muslim men. They forget that polygamy is allowed only under certain social conditions and is a mechanism to achieve social stability. For instance, after major wars a society may have a large number of widows and orphans that have to be taken care of. Similarly in some countries demographic balance is disturbed resulting in a higher number of women as compared to men. Another situation could be that a woman can't bear children for health reasons so instead of divorcing she allows her husband to marry second time. In these situations, there are chances that social ills might emerge in society. In these special circumstances men may marry multiple times but even then, they must discharge their responsibilities with justice and respect. Islam prefers monogamy and considers it a righteous act without exclusively rejecting polygamy. In times of peace if a State regulates a law that imposes restriction on polygamy, restrict approval of polygamy to special family situations or consent of the wife then it will not be against the tenets of Islam.

Many Muslim societies have adopted an attitude that the responsibility of a family or tribe's honor rests solely on the behavior of women while men have a free hand in their endeavors. This perception is wrong; honor is more a responsibility of men in terms of their conduct rather than placing it entirely on the shoulders of women. Chastity and modesty are not just prescribed for women but for men as well.

(Verse 24.030) *Say to the believing men that they should lower their gaze and guard their modesty: that will make for greater purity for them: And Allah is well acquainted with all that they do.*

(Verse 24.031) *And say to the believing women that they should lower their gaze and guard their modesty; that they should not display their beauty and ornaments except what (must ordinarily) appear thereof; that they should draw their veils over their bosoms and not display their beauty except to their husbands, their fathers, their husband's fathers, their sons, their husbands' sons, their brothers or their brothers' sons, or their sisters' sons, or their women, or the slaves whom their right hands possess, or male servants free of physical needs, or small children who have no sense of the shame of sex; and that they should not strike their feet in order to draw attention to their hidden ornaments. And O ye Believers! Turn ye all together towards Allah, that ye may attain Bliss.*

Extravagant exhibition of beauty by women and of their manliness by men is looked down upon in Islamic teachings. Wearing *hijab* (a cloth that covers the face and hair) is a voluntary act by a woman. Men of the family or a State cannot impose it by promulgating a law. Similarly, a State cannot force a woman to abandon their *hijab*, as secular governments in Turkey or France tried to do.

One of the most controversial aspects of women's rights, in Muslim societies, is their right as full citizen to testify in a court of law. Some critics of Islam have presented the view that women are considered half citizens because two women are equal to one man when it comes to testifying in a court of law. There is only one verse that mentions the testimony of two women which is presented here:

(Verse 2.282) *O ye who believe! When ye deal with each other, in transactions involving future obligations in a fixed period of time, reduce them to writing Let a scribe write down faithfully as between the parties: let not the scribe refuse to write: as Allah Has taught him, so let him write. Let him who incurs the liability dictate, but let him fear His Lord Allah, and not diminish aught of what he owes. If the party liable is mentally deficient, or weak, or unable Himself to dictate, Let* *his guardian dictate faithfully, and get two witnesses, out of your own men, and if there are not two men, then a man and two women, such as ye choose, for witnesses, so that if one of them errs, the other can remind her. The witnesses should not refuse when they are called on (For evidence). Disdain not to reduce to writing (your contract) for a future period, whether it be small or big: it is juster in the sight of Allah, More suitable as evidence, and more convenient to prevent doubts among yourselves but if it be a transaction which ye carry out on the spot among yourselves, there is no blame on you if ye reduce it not to writing. But take witness whenever ye make a commercial contract; and let neither scribe nor witness suffer harm. If ye do (such harm), it would be wickedness in you. So fear Allah; For it is Good that teaches you. And Allah is well acquainted with all things. If ye are on a journey, and cannot find a scribe, a pledge with possession (may serve the purpose). And if one of you deposits a thing on trust with another, let the trustee (faithfully) discharge his trust, and let him Fear his Lord conceal not evidence; for whoever conceals it, - his heart is tainted with sin. And Allah knoweth all that ye do.*

As is evident from the verse, it is a specific situation in which two women and a man are required to witness execution of a commercial agreement. Many feminists view it as a women's right issue, but it is recognition of physiological difference between men and women. Men do not have a biological condition when they can be incapacitated to provide evidence like pregnancy and menstrual cycles. Similarly divorced and widowed women have to be restricted to private quarters for a certain time, called *idat*, to ensure they are not pregnant by their former husband. Provision of two women to witness the contract increases the probability that at least one of them is available to provide evidence if required. The verse does not suggest that both women have to be present at the time of provision of evidence. Verse 2.282 is also an indication that justice should not be delayed because of the unavailability of a witness to provide evidence.

Distributing the burden of witness on two women is a blessing from God rather than discrimination against female gender. It is a known fact that during her monthly periods a woman is affected psychological and emotionally. Menstrual periods of a woman are a private matter and are not public information which might be the case at the time of providing evidence in a commercial dispute. A redundancy is created by requiring another woman to witness a contract as well so that at least one of them is available. The other explanation could be that in commercial transaction economic interests are involved which may induce one party to get greedy and force a woman to retrieve or falsify her witness. It is easy to coerce women because of vulnerabilities peculiar to them to provide false evidence than a man. Third situation could be that when a woman is called to provide evidence, she may be in her restricted period imposed on widows and divorce. Or that she is in the last trimester of pregnancy when it is not advisable to put her through duress. Another thing to consider is that witnessing a commercial transaction is a specific situation that is not encountered by all citizens but limited to a small percentage of a community.

From the preceding discussion it is possible that requirement of two women witnessing a contract is not a rights issue but rather a convenience for women to be excused to provide evidence in case one of them are going through a special circumstance that is unique to them. It is highly improbable that both women have the same menstrual cycle or are pregnant at the same time. And if that is the situation then the court has to delay the proceedings until one of the women is available to provide evidence.

Some may raise a question about absence of any women attaining the status of a prophet as a Divine discrimination. There is no exact answer, but two arguments may take the discussion further. First is that human beings tend to grant themselves the status of gods as we have observed in many pagan cultures around the world. Most idol figurines are in the shape of humans. Between the sexes, only women have the capability to rear a child while men can't. This power of creation could have induced people to grant the status of gods to women prophets. We have seen this from the story of Prophet Issa (AS) who had a virgin birth. The other way to look at it is that all prophets went through normal cycles of life; being born to a woman through nine months of pregnancy, being nurtured by women around them in infancy and even in adulthood with their wives working with them to promote their message. They have as much contribution in promoting faith as a Prophet himself without assuming the hardship faced by him. The Quran honors many of these women by narrating their stories.

Sharing

(Verse 2.177) *It is not righteousness that ye turn your faces towards East or West; but it is righteousness- to believe in Allah and the Last Day, and the Angels, and the Book, and the Messengers; to spend of your substance, out of love for Him, for your kin, for orphans, for the needy, for the wayfarer, for those who ask, and for the ransom of slaves; to be steadfast in prayer, and practice regular charity; to fulfill the contracts which ye have made; and to be firm and patient, in pain (or suffering) and adversity, and throughout all periods of panic. Such are the people of truth, the Allah-fearing.*

(Verse 2.215) *They ask thee what they should spend (In charity). Say: Whatever ye spend that is good, is for parents and kindred and orphans and those in want and for wayfarers. And whatever ye do that is good, -Allah knoweth it well.*

(Verse 2.264) *O ye who believe! Cancel not your charity by reminders of your generosity or by injury,- like those who spend their substance to be seen of men, but believe neither in Allah nor in the Last Day. They are in parable like a hard, barren rock, on which is a little soil: on it falls heavy rain, which leaves it (Just) a bare stone. They will be able to do nothing with aught they have earned. And Allah guideth not those who reject faith.*

(Verse 2.267) *O ye who believe! Give of the good things which ye have (honorably) earned, and of the fruits of the earth which We have produced for you, and do not even aim at getting anything which is bad, in order that out of it ye may give away something, when ye yourselves would not receive it except with closed eyes. And know that Allah is Free of all wants, and worthy of all praise.*

(Verse 2.271) *If ye disclose (acts of) charity, even so it is well, but if ye conceal them, and make them reach those (really) in need, that is best for you: It will remove from you some of your (stains of) evil. And Allah is well acquainted with what ye do.*

(Verse 2.273) *(Charity is) for those in need, who, in Allah's cause are restricted (from travel), and cannot move about in the land, seeking (For trade or work): the ignorant man thinks, because of their modesty, that they are free from want. Thou* *shalt know them by their (Unfailing) mark: They beg not importunately from all the sundry. And whatever of good ye give, be assured Allah knoweth it well.*

(Verse 4.036) *Serve Allah, and join not any partners with Him; and do good- to parents, kinsfolk, orphans, those in need, neighbors who are near, neighbors who are strangers, the companion by your side, the wayfarer (ye meet), and what your right hands possess: For Allah loveth not the arrogant, the vainglorious;-*

(Verse 9.060) *Alms are for the poor and the needy, and those employed to administer the (funds); for those whose hearts have been (recently) reconciled (to Truth); for those in bondage and in debt; in the cause of Allah; and for the wayfarer: (thus is it) ordained by Allah, and Allah is full of knowledge and wisdom.*

(Verse 47.038) *Behold, ye are those invited to spend (of your substance) in the Way of Allah: But among you are some that are niggardly. But any who are niggardly are so at the expense of their own souls. But Allah is free of all wants, and it is ye that are needy. If ye turn back (from the Path), He will substitute in your stead another people; then they would not be like you!*

Voluntary acts of charity not only create goodwill among citizens but also reduce income inequality that has been the prime mover of many revolutions around the world. Islam encourages people to share their prosperity, with others, by engaging in voluntary acts of charity (*sadaqa*) that is apart from the mandatory charity of *zakat*. It advises that a person should help his family members, neighbors and even travelers that might need it while passing through a town. The Islamic concept of sharing encourages active participation in managing operations of a charitable organization instead of being a passive donor by just writing a cheque. People who do not have money to contribute to charity are advised to share their time and expertise with the community.

A person has the right to give to charity openly or secretly which requires that laws governing regulation of non-profit charitable trusts should respect privacy by offering both options. Islam encourages that people can spend as much as they desire in charity that is beyond their needs. This creates circulation of wealth in the community which has its own economic benefits in terms of generating employment and increasing demand. A unique concept presented by Islam is that spending money in charity contributes to increasing the wealth of a person but also adds to blessings in hereafter. In economic terms it could be interpreted that keeping money in circulation makes the economy grow rather than keeping assets frozen in bank accounts or non-productive property like piece of land.

Islamic Social Contract combines life on earth and hereafter in all our actions. Charity is one of the most mentioned individual deeds of good behavior in the Quran that is a key stone of a socially just society. The Quran instructs to distribute charity in a manner that maintains dignity of the recipients. Islam recognizes that an honorable person in need may not be seeking financial help to maintain their self-respect. It is incumbent on a community to be cognizant of the needs of their members and reach out to them first. Congregating for prayers in a mosque five times a day is an avenue for people to know each other and share the burden of hardship with those who are going through a crisis.

Islam recognizes that a portion of the charity can be spent on people who are engaged in its management (verse 9.060) but it is expected that the motive of these people should not be to have an income rather they should be driven by the passion to serve the community. This will earn them a reward in the afterlife as well as have a decent income in the world. Islam honors people that engage in charity management by bestowing them with high social stature and respect rather than an elevated financial status. In the Islamic concept of charity, the chief executive of UNICEF or Red Cross cannot earn an income that is many folds higher than the average salary in a community. By permitting to spend a portion of donations on the administrative management, Islam promotes institutionalization of charitable organization on non-profit basis which can have profound effect in alleviating poverty and other forms of social oppression in a society.

It is important to note that the focus of charity should be local rather than national. This means that the first preference of any charity is to help their local community (verse 2.177, 2.215 & 4.036) to ensure that all members have access to basic needs of life such as food, shelter and clothing. The extent of charity in terms of who is eligible are defined in the Quranic verses, but the scope of charity is open in terms of for which causes it can be used. This is an important distinction to remember because the use of charity will depend on the relative economic and social development of a community. In a relatively low-income country with wide income inequality charity can be spent to reduce those inequalities. On the other hand, in prosperous countries charity can help find cures for diseases that are prevalent in a community, or it can be used to set up schools and hospitals for the poor. Frequent mentioning of charity in the Quranic verses makes it clear that provision of social services is as much the responsibility of community members as much as it is the responsibility of the State.

Interestingly the Quran does not mention that the person to whom charity is given should be a believer rather it only mentions that they are neighbors, friends, family and even strangers passing through the city. There is a misconception among Muslims that charity should be distributed among believers only. In a Muslim neighborhood there could be non-Muslim families that are in need. Quran instructs to help a neighbor without discriminating based on their religion, so a non-Muslim should not be deprived of charity because of their religion. Charity is meant to enable the creation of a socially just society which is the only sure way to live by the faith.

Rights to Privacy & Transparency

(Verse 2.189) *They ask thee concerning the New Moons. Say: They are but signs to mark fixed periods of time in (the affairs of) men, and for Pilgrimage. It is no virtue if ye enter your houses from the back: It is virtue if ye fear Allah. Enter houses through the proper doors: And fear Allah: That ye may prosper.*

(Verse 2.263) *Kind words and the covering of faults are better than charity followed by injury. Allah is free of all wants, and He is Most-Forbearing.*

(Verse 24.019) *Those who love (to see) scandal published broadcast among the Believers, will have a grievous Penalty in this life and in the Hereafter: Allah knows, and ye know not.*

(Verse 24.027) *O ye who believe! enter not houses other than your own, until ye have asked permission and saluted those in them: that is best for you, in order that* *ye may heed (what is seemly).* ***(Verse 24.028)*** *If ye find no one in the house, enter not until permission is given to you: if ye are asked to go back, go back: that makes for greater purity for yourselves: and Allah knows well all that ye do.*

(Verse 49.006) *O ye who believe! If a wicked person comes to you with any news, ascertain the truth, lest ye harm people unwittingly, and afterwards become full of repentance for what ye have done.*

(Verse 49.012) *O ye who believe! Avoid suspicion as much (as possible): for suspicion in some cases is a sin: And spy not on each other behind their backs. Would any of you like to eat the flesh of his dead brother? Nay, ye would abhor it... But fear Allah: For Allah is Oft-Returning, Most Merciful.*

(Verse 58.010) *Secret counsels are only (inspired) by the Evil One, in order that he may cause grief to the Believers; but he cannot harm them in the least, except as Allah permits; and on Allah let the Believers put their trust.*

(Verse 104.001) *Woe to every (kind of) scandal-monger and-backbiter,*

The Universal Bill of Rights was adopted in 1948 when the United Nations (UN) was established but fourteen centuries earlier and for the first time in civilized history a religion mandated that people have a right to privacy. The preceding verses provide an insight into the Islamic ideal of privacy which can be summed up as follows:

1. Each person has a right to privacy even among family members
2. Citizens are expected to maintain respect and dignity for each other by abstaining from spreading rumors, and abuse personal weaknesses and avoid seeking undisclosed information behind each other's back
3. In dealing with each other people should be upfront and transparent rather than conspire to gain unethical advantage over each other.

The State as an arbiter has to ensure that the privacy of every citizen is protected, and violators are prosecuted. The State does not have the right to spy on its citizens or seek information without explicit permission from courts to do so. The State has to ensure that private information of its citizens, for example birth certificates, property records, and tax collections, are protected from leakage and abuse. Officials within various State functions are expected not to share private information of citizens without explicit permission from the courts. Evidence collected without knowledge of the people is not admissible in a court of law for purpose of prosecution or claiming of damages. Organizations holding personal information of people, for instance doctors, lawyers and accountants, have to be compliant with the principles of privacy.

Maintaining Order & Discipline

(Verse 2.084) *And remember We took your covenant (to this effect): Shed no blood amongst you, nor turn out your own people from your homes: and this ye solemnly ratified, and to this ye can bear witness.*

(Verse 4.059) *O ye who believe! Obey Allah, and obey the Messenger, and those charged with authority among you. If ye differ in anything among yourselves, refer it to Allah and His Messenger, if ye do believe in Allah and the Last Day: That is best, and most suitable for final determination.*

(Verse 4.083) *When there comes to them some matter touching (Public) safety or fear, they divulge it. If they had only referred it to the Messenger, or to those charged with authority among them, the proper investigators would have tested it from them (direct). Were it not for the Grace and Mercy of Allah unto you, all but a few of you would have fallen into the clutches of Satan.*

(Verse 7.056) *Do no mischief on the earth, after it hath been set in order, but call on Him with fear and longing (in your hearts): for the Mercy of Allah is (always) near to those who do good.*

(Verse 42.042) *The blame is only against those who oppress men and wrong-doing and insolently transgress beyond bounds through the land, defying right and justice: for such there will be a penalty grievous.* ***(Verse 42.043)*** *But indeed if any show patience and forgive, that would truly be an exercise of courageous will and resolution in the conduct of affairs.*

Quote from last sermon of Prophet Mohammad (PBUH):

"O People, just as you regard this month, this day, this city as Sacred, so regard the life and property of every Muslim as a sacred trust. Return the goods entrusted to you to their rightful owners. Hurt no one so that no one may hurt you."

The Islamic social state requires that all its citizens respect local laws and regulations. Islam loathes anarchy and the breakdown of order. It offers a systemic removal of those engaged in corruption and abuse of power. This is achieved through removing indemnity for all officers of the State including the chief executive of the government. Secondly Islam requires citizens to raise their voice when they witness an injustice or corruption even if they feel a threat to their life, family or property. The Quran makes it clear that those that die in protest to prevent an injustice are granted special favors in the afterlife. Islam grants political leaders' authority through an allegiance of all citizens which in contemporary times is earned in the form of a popular democratic mandate. This political power should be used by leaders to establish a just society and suppress oppression.

Some scholars have interpreted verses 4.059 & 4.083 to mean that people have to even obey rulers that are corrupt and oppressive. These same verses were used to validate monarchies and autocrats. This is a misconception. Allocation of political power is discussed in detail in chapter 3, but it is important to note here that citizens of the State are required to raise their voice against corruption and oppression but in an orderly fashion rather than resorting to anarchy and riots. There are many steps suggested to raise a voice against corruption. These include filing petitions against rulers in a court of law. If a court is unable to contain corruption, then people should come together to create civic organizations that can contain the influence of corrupt authorities. Social issues have to be brought to the notice of city administrators through collective action rather than people resorting to taking the law in their own hands or breaking public property in demonstrations.

There has been substantial debate among Muslim scholars that people of authority referred to in many Quranic verses are experts in *Sharia* law and tenets of Islam. This is a narrow definition. A consensus has emerged over many centuries of scholarly discourse that people of authority could be referring to different sets of people depending on the situation. Political authority resides with elected officials. Religious authority is with scholars and educators. Administrative authority is with city administrators and functionaries. Legal authority is with *Qadis* (judges) and magistrates. In an Islamic Social State constitution defines boundaries of these authorities which have to be respected by all citizens. To maintain law and order the Islamic idea is that each function of the society should work within their framework and not impinge on the authority of the other.

National Security

*(**Verse 3.169**) Think not of those who are slain in Allah's way as dead. Nay, they live, finding their sustenance in the presence of their Lord; (**Verse 3.170**) They rejoice in the bounty provided by Allah: And with regard to those left behind, who have not yet joined them (in their bliss), the (Martyrs) glory in the fact that on them is no fear, nor have they (cause to) grieve.*

*(**Verse 4.095**) Not equal are those believers who sit (at home) and receive no hurt, and those who strive and fight in the cause of Allah with their goods and their persons. Allah hath granted a grade higher to those who strive and fight with their goods and persons than to those who sit (at home). Unto all (in Faith) Hath Allah promised good: But those who strive and fight Hath He distinguished above those who sit (at home) by a special reward,-*

*(**Verse 9.020**) Those who believe, and suffer exile and strive with might and main, in Allah's cause, with their goods and their persons, have the highest rank in the sight of Allah: they are the people who will achieve (salvation).*

*(**Verse 9.041**) Go ye forth, (whether equipped) lightly or heavily, and strive and struggle, with your goods and your persons, in the cause of Allah. That is best for you, if ye (but) knew.*

*(**Verse 9.044**) Those who believe in Allah and the Last Day ask thee for no exemption from fighting with their goods and persons. And Allah knoweth well those who do their duty.*

*(**Verse 9.052**) Say: "Can you expect for us (any fate) other than one of two glorious things- (Martyrdom or victory)? But we can expect for you either that Allah will send his punishment from Himself, or by our hands. So wait (expectant); we too will wait with you."*

*(**Verse 16.041**) To those who leave their homes in the cause of Allah, after*

suffering oppression,- We will assuredly give a goodly home in this world; but truly the reward of the Hereafter will be greater. If they only realized (this)!

(Verse 29.002) *Do men think that they will be left alone on saying, "We believe", and that they will not be tested?*

(Verse 48.017) *No blame is there on the blind, nor is there blame on the lame, nor on one ill (if he joins not the war): But he that obeys Allah and his Messenger,- (Allah) will admit him to Gardens beneath which rivers flow; and he who turns back, (Allah) will punish him with a grievous Penalty.*

(Verse 49.009) *If two parties among the Believers fall into a quarrel, make ye peace between them: but if one of them transgresses beyond bounds against the other, then fight ye (all) against the one that transgresses until it complies with the command of Allah; but if it complies, then make peace between them with justice, and be fair: for Allah loves those who are fair (and just).*

The objective of an Islamic Social State is to establish a just society. This objective cannot be achieved unless all members of the community contribute towards it. The Islamic concept of state security has two dimensions. One relates to internal stability by standing up to oppression and injustice as well as to engage in charity to reduce social and economic inequalities. In a State that has a diversity of cultures it is expected that justice and fairness will be practiced by all. In case one community engages in an injustice against another, that could damage the social balance, then all other communities have to unite to ensure that justice prevails, and social balance is regained (Verse 49.009).

The other dimension is securing the community from external aggression. In an Islamic Social State, it is expected that all healthy individuals will join the struggle for state security if called upon by those in authority. Citizens that are disabled are given exemption. There is no exception to this rule for all healthy and able-bodied citizens. State has to ensure that citizens are provided basic training in civil defense including border security, community police, ambulance operations and firefighting. In times of peace members of the State are expected to make financial contributions towards funding adequate military expenses to keep adversaries at bay.

Organizing Society

Sovereignty

*(**Verse** 2.107) Knowest thou not that to Allah belongeth the dominion of the heavens and the earth? And besides Him ye have neither patron nor helper.*

*(**Verse** 7.185) Do they see nothing in the government of the heavens and the earth and all that Allah hath created? (Do they not see) that it may well be that their terms is nigh drawing to an end? In what message after this will they then believe?*

*(**Verse 13.002**) Allah is He Who raised the heavens without any pillars that ye can see; is firmly established on the throne (of authority); He has subjected the sun and the moon (to his Law)! Each one runs (its course) for a term appointed. He doth regulate all affairs, explaining the signs in detail, that ye may believe with certainty in the meeting with your Lord.*

*(**Verse 23.088**) Say: "Who is it in whose hands is the governance of all things,- who protects (all), but is not protected (of any)? (say) if ye know." (**Verse 23.089**) They will say, "(It belongs) to Allah." Say: "Then how are ye deluded?"*

*(**Verse 25.002**) He to whom belongs the dominion of the heavens and the earth: no son has He begotten, nor has He a partner in His dominion: it is He who created all things, and ordered them in due proportions.*

*(**Verse 32.005**) He rules (all) affairs from the heavens to the earth: in the end will (all affairs) go up to Him, on a Day, the space whereof will be (as) a thousand years of your reckoning.*

The sovereignty of God is all encompassing even beyond the reaches of this earth, which is just a small part of a vast universe. The sovereignty of men, on the other hand, is limited only to the temporal matters while spiritual matters are exclusively in God's domain. The temporal authority of men is derived from his designation as *Khalifa* (vice-regent) on earth as well as the free will expressed through freedom of religion. If it was a Divine Will to control the actions of men, then God would not grant free will to men as well as the liberty to commit *shirk* (to share) by ascribing partners with Him. In worldly affairs all mankind is equal in the eyes of God regardless of whether they believe in Him or not because if it was not true then non-Muslims would not be able to get sustenance and prosperity. God has relegated the punishment of *Shirk* (associating partners with God) to an afterlife. Non-believers are not judged in this world for their inability to find a true faith but rather they have to answer for their sins towards God in the afterlife. The following verses make it clear that even Prophet Mohammad (PBUH) cannot compel people to accept Islam as their religion.

(Verse 2.256) *Let there be no compulsion in religion: Truth stands out clear from Error: whoever rejects evil and believes in Allah hath grasped the most trustworthy hand-hold, that never breaks. And Allah heareth and knoweth all things.*

(Verse 2.272) *It is not required of thee (O Messenger), to set them on the right path, but Allah sets on the right path whom He pleaseth. Whatever of good ye give benefits your own souls, and ye shall only do so seeking the "Face" of Allah. Whatever good ye give, shall be rendered back to you, and ye shall not be dealt with unjustly.*

(Verse 6.035) *If their spurning is hard on thy mind, yet if thou wert able to seek a tunnel in the ground or a ladder to the skies and bring them a sign,- (what good?). If it were Allah's will, He could gather them together unto true guidance: so be not thou amongst those who are swayed by ignorance (and impatience)!*

These are just a small sample of numerous Quranic verses that makes it clear that spiritual sovereignty is an exclusive domain of God and no one has the right to interfere in it. Freedom of religion or faith is one of the basic rights granted to men by God, the State cannot adopt an official religion although it is anticipated that in a Muslim majority country the social values are derived from tenets of Quran and *Sunnah* (tradition) of Prophet Mohammad (PBUH).

It is not the State that is Muslim but the individuals that reside in it. In Islamic concept a State is not an entity by itself but emerges out of the free will of people to come together to form a community. The objective of a State, as an administrative entity, is to manage the affairs of this community so that they have a good quality of life on earth and salvation in an afterlife. A State cannot decide for its citizens which religion to follow or not follow but leave it to the individual citizens to decide. The State is neutral in terms of dictating religious matters but encourages its citizens to have faith by including religious education in the school curriculum.

(Verse 6.165) *It is He Who hath made you (His) agents, inheritors of the earth: He hath raised you in ranks, some above others: that He may try you in the gifts He hath given you: for thy Lord is quick in punishment: yet He is indeed Oft-forgiving, Most Merciful.*

(Verse 7.010) *It is We Who have placed you with authority on earth, and provided you therein with means for the fulfillment of your life: small are the thanks that ye give!*

(Verse 7.181) *Of those We have created are people who direct (others) with truth. And dispense justice therewith.*

(Verse 35.039) *He it is That has made you inheritors in the earth: if, then, any do reject (Allah), their rejection (works) against themselves: their rejection but adds to the odium for the Unbelievers in the sight of their Lord: their rejection but adds to (their own) undoing.*

The sovereignty of men in temporal matters is evident from the free will God has granted to Adam and his progeny. The status of *Khalifa* (vice-regent) manifests in temporal sovereignty which is an integral component of human condition regardless of adherence to any one particular religion. In the Islamic concept of society sovereignty belongs to all citizens rather than to a particular office of a State or an outside agency such as a constitution as presented by secularism. Legislators have been given agency by the voters to formulate laws, based on their expertise, but it is the people that have the final word to approve or reject the proposed laws. No legislation that will have an impact on social values or provision of justice can be passed until it is directly voted upon by the members of the community. In this concept the members of the legislative assembly can draft a law that has an impact on basic human rights, granted by God, but it has to be ratified by the community through a direct vote. Laws that are related to operations of a state for instance, increase in budget expenditure or balance of power between various political institutions can be adopted by the legislature. But even those laws can be challenged by the citizens, by filing a petition in a court of law, if they feel it could have an adverse effect on social justice. This procedure is practiced by many States in United States where a law is voted in a general election to be approved by the people.

The legislature has to ensure that proposed laws do not impinge on the social values and individual liberties granted to people by Quran and *Sunnah*. In an Islamic concept no agency has the absolute authority to claim overriding right to define the Divine Will. Any laws that curtail freedom of religion or impose a certain version of a faith cannot be promulgated as it is against the liberties granted to men by God. Another example is that if the State provides religious education in public schools or mandates it for private schools to include it in their curriculum then all religions that are part of a community have to be included on the curriculum. On the other hand, if legislation prohibits use of pork, alcohol and interest within the boundaries of a State and it is approved by a majority then it is incumbent upon all citizens to adhere to it regardless of their faith. Prohibition of these does not curtail quality of life and can be replaced by other alternatives available. One important parameter to consider when prohibiting alcohol or pork is that no law can take away the right of privacy of a person in terms of their behavior. A person consuming alcohol in the privacy of his home without including others or making public appearance while intoxicated has to be treated differently because of his right of privacy. There was an incident reported that Caliph Umer while patrolling the streets heard noises coming out of a house. He suspected drunkenness and scaled the walls of the house to apprehend the culprits. When the case was brought before a *Qadi (judges)*, he reprimanded the Caliph for unlawfully collecting the evidence by impinging on the privacy of a citizen while the culprits were acquitted because evidence was collected unlawfully. Even in secular countries there are restrictions on smoking or driving while intoxicated. It is the collective responsibility of the community to ensure that basic rights of each citizen are protected that are granted to them by the Quran and *Sunnah* as outlined in Chapter 2 of this book.

The sovereignty is granted to citizens rather than an assembly of elected representative because Islam encourages people to be actively engaged in matters of community. Secular democracy takes away that right once they cast their votes and transfer their agency to legislate to elected parliamentarians. In an Islamic State draft legislation have to be approved by a majority through an election process. It is expected that the individuals will be well informed of the issues and understand the social values promoted by Islam. Religious scholars have to educate people about Islamic social values, but they do not have the sovereign right to promulgate laws. Blame for any transgressions of basic rights is a burden on the whole community rather than a handful of legislative assembly members. Since sovereignty belongs to the community at large and that there is no sanctioned religious authority to define the injunctions of Islamic social values, no one section of society has the right to claim authority to interpreting the social tenets of Islam. As Prophet himself said "My community will never agree in error."

Constitution

In an Islamic Social State, the constitution is an operating document that upholds the social values offered by the Quran and *Sunnah* of Prophet Mohammad (PBUH). The constitution contains following:

1. It outlines the rights of citizens derived from Quran and *Sunnah* of Prophet Mohammad (PBUH) (refer to chapter 2)
2. Outlines qualifications, roles and responsibilities of the chief executive, cabinet members, parliament and judiciary
3. Procedure to nominate, elect and impeach elected representatives
4. Create balance of power between executive, legislative and judicial branches of the government

The constitution in an Islamic state is not a static document. Apart from routine constitutional amendments, it has to be reviewed periodically to accommodate social changes in society. To institutionalize this process the constitution can incorporate an article to have a comprehensive review after a lapse of one or two generations i.e. 30 or 60 years. This review has to be conducted by a constituent assembly that is elected for this purpose. The amendments suggested by this constituent assembly have to be ratified through a majority vote of 50% plus one when the voter turnout is at least 51% of the total registered voters. Failure to achieve this threshold will nullify the amendments proposed by the constituent assembly.

Structure & Scope of Government

The Quran and the *Sunnah* (tradition) of Prophet Mohammad (PBUH) do not suggest any preferred design of the government. In a way this was a blessing because a divinely ordained or prophetically sanctified structure of government could not be amended by later generations. It is evident from Quranic Verse 13.11 ***Allah does not change a people's lot unless they change what is in their hearts***.

The Quran recognizes that human condition is evolutionary. To accommodate the evolutionary nature of a society a government structure has to go through period reviews and adjustments. It has been left to the community to organize their affairs according to their local environment. Any government structure that supports and enables social values presented in Chapter 2 is acceptable. Apart from that, a government structure has to ensure that

1. Will of the people is not curtailed by monopolizing the power in an individual or a group,
2. Transfer of power should be based on mandate and allegiance of community,
3. Decisions should be made through consultation and,
4. Social justice must prevail.

There is no evidence of establishing mandatory Caliphate ruling all of the Muslim *Ummah* (community) by the Quran or *Sunnah*.

(Verse 2.148) *To each is a goal to which Allah turns him; then strive together (as in a race) Towards all that is good. Wheresoever ye are, Allah will bring you Together. For Allah Hath power over all things.*

(Verse 10.019) *Mankind was but one nation, but differed (later). Had it not been for a word that went forth before from thy Lord, their differences would have been settled between them.*

(Verse 11.118) *If thy Lord had so willed, He could have made mankind one people: but they will not cease to dispute.*

(Verse 13.011) *For each (such person) there are (angels) in succession, before and behind him: They guard him by command of Allah. Allah does not change a people's lot unless they change what is in their hearts. But when (once) Allah willeth a people's punishment, there can be no turning it back, nor will they find, besides Him, any to protect.*

(Verse 16.093) *If Allah so willed, He could make you all one people: But He leaves straying whom He pleases, and He guides whom He pleases: but ye shall certainly be called to account for all your actions.*

(Verse 22.067) *To every People have We appointed rites and ceremonies which they must follow: let them not then dispute with thee on the matter, but do thou invite (them) to thy Lord: for thou art assuredly on the Right Way.*

(Verse 42.008) *If Allah had so willed, He could have made them a single people; but He admits whom He will to His Mercy; and the Wrong-doers will have no protector nor helper.*

(Verse 49.013) *O mankind! We created you from a single (pair) of a male and a female, and made you into nations and tribes, that ye may know each other (not that ye may despise (each other). Verily the most honored of you in the sight of Allah is (he who is) the most righteous of you. And Allah has full knowledge and is well acquainted (with all things).*

The preceding verses suggest preference for a government that manages a local community in which social values promoted by Islam are upheld. A State is formed when a group voluntarily comes together because of geographical, cultural, religious and economic affinity towards each other. This State is then managed by leaders that are elected by people through popular vote. This fact of local responsibilities is also reflected in Islamic rituals. The Islamic ritual of Hajj, when Muslims from all over the world gather at Mecca to interact as well as worship with each other, is required to be performed once in a lifetime. On the other hand, *salat* (prayer) is performed five times a day in a local mosque; mandatory charity zakat is distributed to help the local community and *sadaqa* (voluntary charity) is advised to be spent on family, neighbors and those around us. This proves that first preference is given to organizing local community or national State. *Ummah,* on the other hand, is a pan-Islamic collaboration of the States to cooperate and collaborate in education, commerce, security and culture. This collaboration does not mandate political cohesion as well but can take the shape of organizations like the European Union (EU) and the Association of Southeast Asian Nations (ASEAN). Organization of Islamic Cooperation (OIC) is a good platform to develop the *Ummah*. These organizations promote commercial and security cooperation but maintain unique cultural heritage and political sovereignty of each nation state.

The government of an Islamic state comprise of the following organs:

1. ***Amir ul Muluk (President/Chief Executive)***: Amir ul Muluk (President) is elected by the people through direct elections outlined in the constitution. Powers of the Amir are extensive in an Islamic State in terms of collecting revenue, allocating government resources, appointing government functionaries, managing foreign affairs and securing the State. The Amir is expected to uphold the social values presented in Chapter 2 in all his actions and executive orders. Citizens have the right to question the actions of the head of government by filing a complaint petition with the judiciary. The Judiciary and *Majlis-e-Shura* (parliament) cannot remove an executive from office. The right of impeachment of the Executive is granted to the citizens who can submit a petition to *Majlis-e-Shura* to seek removal of an Amir from office and call new elections before the expiration of his term of office. A term limit can be imposed for holding the office of Amir to avoid nepotism

and cronyism taking root in society.

2. ***Executive Cabinet/Ministers/Vizier***: The elected Amir should have authority to appoint his cabinet. Nominations should be based on merit and may not necessarily be members of *Majlis-e-Shura* (legislative assembly). In the case nomination of a cabinet member is from among *Majlis-e-Shura* then that person has to resign from his parliamentary seat to avoid conflict of interest arising from holding two offices. The Islamic idea of responsibility rejects any kind of conflict of interest so that a member of *Majlis-e-shura* that joins a cabinet has to relinquish their membership of legislature. This enables division of responsibilities, avoids conflict of interest as well as safeguarding public interest at all levels. The Amir should be mindful that his cabinet reflects the diversity of the community. The constitution may give *Majlis-e-Shura* powers to ratify cabinet nominees before they can be sworn to office. The constitution can grant people the right to recall a cabinet member if they feel he is engaging in corruption or is not effective in discharging his responsibilities. This right was exercised frequently by people during the time of *Rashidun* (rightly guided) Caliphs when governors were removed from office because of frequent complaints. The conditions for recall in case of a cabinet position should involve evidence from experts that the Minister was not been able to manage affairs of a particular department. If the court accepts their case, then the Amir has to replace that person.
3. ***Majlis-e-shura (Parliament)*** or legislative assembly. It could be unicameral or bicameral depending on the unique social, cultural and economic profile of a State. These are all elected members by popular vote according to the process outlined by the constitution. Citizens should have the right to recall their representative by filing a petition with the speaker of *Majlis-e-Shura*. Conditions for recall or impeachment should be made part of the Constitution. These could include corruption, nepotism, and failure to uphold the trust of the people, abuse of power or transgressing the basic rights of people. The constitution should provide an adequate hurdle to cross to avoid abusive use of recall clause. It may

be required that a certain percentage of registered voters sign a petition to recall a parliamentarian. A Member of Parliament is automatically recalled if a guilty verdict is awarded by a court in a criminal or civil case filed against that member.

4. ***Qadis (Judiciary)*** are appointed by the Amir but approved by *Majlis-e-shura* to create a balance of power between the institutions of the government. Once appointed executive and legislative branches cannot influence decisions of the *Qadis*.
5. ***Local Government***: This includes provincial and city administrators. These are elected by local communities to manage their affairs. These representatives serve their communities but have to pledge allegiance to the Amir to legitimize their actions as part of a State as well as to reduce friction between these centers of power. By pledging allegiance to the Amir, local government officials agree to accept the powers of the national constitution and form a federation with the center.
6. ***Government Departments***: These are salaried bureaucrats that administer the government functions. These appointments should be made based on the criteria of merit, honesty and integrity. To maintain social justice in a diverse community, fair representations of all ethnicities have to be ensured.

The dual system of head of state and chief executive emerged from constitutional monarchy in which Monarch would become head of state, representing sovereignty, while Prime Minister became the chief executive, managing affairs of government. In many countries, where a federation is formed between republics, like United States of America, the President represents the sovereignty of the people as head of government. The Islamic system of government offers a unified system of government in which all layers of government operate under one constitution and subservient to the people. In an Islamic State sovereignty lies with the people while elected representatives have the executive and legislative authority to conduct affairs of the state.

An Islamic State with a culturally diverse community has to accept faith as a string that unites the pearls. Federating units do not have their own rights as a separate entity but are administrative units to ensure development of their local communities. These units have to be reorganized if some of them grow too big to be managed efficiently by local administrations. Creation of provinces on ethnic lines is not supported by the Islamic values of community building. Islam recognizes culture as an integral part of a person's identity but at the same time reject it as a political entity that can supersede the interests of the community at large. A good example is, Charter of Medinah when various tribes, that had been fighting each other for generations, came together to form one community by dissolving the political rights of individual tribes. Even the election of the first Caliph Abu Bakr (RATA) was based on the idea of preserving the State instead of protecting the rights of a particular segment of the community. The State has to recognize and support various cultures within its boundaries but cannot sow seeds of division by granting them political rights by creating provinces based on ethnic interests. To create a homogeneous community, Islam encourages cross cultural marriages and free flow of people and capital between Muslim communities.

In an Islamic state the role of government is limited to be a referee, to provide a level playing field to all its citizens. The government has to be small because it should not engage itself in provision of social services or development of infrastructure. These roles are given to the local government representatives. Functions of government, in an Islamic Social State, are:

1. Securing borders of the State against foreign aggressors
2. Conduct foreign policy to form alliances and execute treaties with other States
3. Ensure compliance to social values (chapter 2), application of social justice and provision of equal opportunity for all citizens.
4. Impose and collect taxes and tariffs to finance state expenses.
5. Ensure provision of speedy and affordable justice throughout the State.

The State cannot engage in competing with private enterprises by creating commercial for-profit public corporations. The State also has to respect private property rights. Provision of social services like health care and education is the responsibility of local governments. They can form non-governmental and non-profit organizations in which wealthy individuals and residents participate on a self-help basis (more on this subject in Chapter 4). The function of the State is to regulate the activities of these organizations as well as to become a last resort to cover deficits that might occur in some low-income or underdeveloped areas.

Amir ul Muluk (President)

*(**Verse 3.026**) Say: "O Allah! Lord of Power (And Rule), Thou givest power to whom Thou pleasest, and Thou strippest off power from whom Thou pleasest: Thou enduest with honour whom Thou pleasest, and Thou bringest low whom Thou pleasest: In Thy hand is all good. Verily, over all things Thou hast power.*

*(**Verse 3.104**) Let there arise out of you a band of people inviting to all that is good, enjoining what is right, and forbidding what is wrong: they are the ones to attain felicity. (**Verse 3.105**) Be not like those who are divided amongst themselves and fall into disputations after receiving Clear Signs: For them is a dreadful penalty,-*

*(**Verse 4.059**) O ye who believe! Obey Allah, and obey the Messenger, and those charged with authority among you. If ye differ in anything among yourselves, refer it to Allah and His Messenger, if ye do believe in Allah and the Last Day: That is best, and most suitable for final determination.*

*(**Verse 6.165**) It is He Who hath made you (His) agents, inheritors of the earth: He hath raised you in ranks, some above others: that He may try you in the gifts He hath given you: for thy Lord is quick in punishment: yet He is indeed Oft-forgiving, Most Merciful.*

*(**Verse 7.128**) Said Moses to his people: "Pray for help from Allah, and (wait) in patience and constancy: for the earth is Allah's, to give as a heritage to such of His servants as He pleaseth; and the end is (best) for the righteous.*

*(**Verse 7.181**) Of those We have created are people who direct (others) with truth. And dispense justice therewith.*

*(**Verse 24.055**) Allah has promised, to those among you who believe and work righteous deeds, that He will, of a surety, grant them in the land, inheritance (of power), as He granted it to those before them; that He will establish in authority*

their religion - the one which He has chosen for them; and that He will change (their state), after the fear in which they (lived), to one of security and peace: 'They will worship Me (alone) and not associate aught with Me. 'If any do reject Faith after this, they are rebellious and wicked.

(Verse 49.013) *O mankind! We created you from a single (pair) of a male and a female, and made you into nations and tribes, that ye may know each other (not that ye may despise (each other). Verily the most honored of you in the sight of Allah is (he who is) the most righteous of you. And Allah has full knowledge and is well acquainted (with all things).*

Sahih Bukhari Hadith #619: *Narrated 'Abdur-Rahman bin Samura: The Prophet said, "O 'Abdur-Rahman bin Samura! Do not seek to be a ruler, because if you are given authority for it, then you will be held responsible for it, but if you are given it without asking for it, then you will be helped in it (by Allah): and whenever you take an oath to do something and later you find that something else is better than the first, then do the better one and make expiation for your oath."*

Citizens are expected to compare candidates for the position of Amir ul Muluk on the following criteria:

1. Demonstrable evidence to uphold justice
2. Trust worthiness and truthfulness
3. Exhibit principled and ethical behavior in public and private dealings
4. Possess and exhibit knowledge and wisdom
5. Practice moderation in their lifestyle
6. Demonstrable political ability to manage affairs of people

To acquire these qualities a person has to have a certain level of experience in life so it's preferable they are of middle age. Candidates cannot promote themselves through speeches and corner meetings. People that have interacted with them in their professional, personal and family life have to come forward to provide evidence of character during the nomination process. Promoters of the candidates should develop detailed profiles of their nominees and distribute them through mass and social media to campaign for their suitability over other contestants.

The Islamic State offers unprecedented executive authority to an Amir to manage the affairs of government. An Amir-elect has to honor and respect the decisions made by the retiring Amir. All treaties and inter-State agreements are upheld until their term expires, abrogated by the other party and/or successfully renegotiated between the parties. The limitations on the authority of an Amir are not to transgress social values outlined in the constitution. He has the authority to select his team based on attributes of merit, credibility, experience and knowledge. While choosing his team the Amir (President) has to ensure that his cabinet should reflect the diversity of the community and is not favorable towards one particular group. Many historians of Islamic history, Arab and non-Arab, have suggested that the rightly guided Caliph Usman (RATA) favored members of *Bani Umayyah* tribe, of which he was a member, in awarding appointments across the State. They further suggest that it was because of this political influence that a war later broke out between Caliph Ali (RATA) and governor of Syria, Amir Muawiyah who was member of *Bani Umayyah* clan, who refused to pledge his allegiance to the new caliph. This endangered the unity of the community and fractured the bond that is hurting the Muslim *Ummah* until this day. We see similar conflicts occur time and again, within Muslim communities, when social justice is not upheld in distributing political power. It is not possible to have a perfect distribution of positions, among a diverse group, but substantial negligence or favor of one or more groups can create dissension and political instability. The American Presidential form of government is quite close to Islamic concept of government except that legislature constrains the influence of the executive authority.

Islam does not exclude descendants of a retiring Amir to be eligible for elected office but nomination and mandate from majority of citizens is the preferred method of transfer of power. Prophet Mohammad (PBUH) did not nominate or designated anyone to succeed him after his death. In a similar fashion none of the rightly guided Caliphs Abu Bakr, Umar, Usman or Ali nominated their descendants as candidates or heirs for political power. The name of Abu Bakr as successor was suggested by Umar in a tribal meeting. At his death bed, Caliph Abu Bakr nominated Umar as his choice but subjected it to the condition that he had to earn the allegiance of people. When Caliph Umar was fatally stabbed, he designated a council of six men to choose from among each other which resulted in the succession of Usman as third Caliph. When Caliph Usman was assassinated, Hazrat Ali was chosen by a community meeting in the central mosque of Medinah. This made Hazrat Ali (RATA) to become the first popularly elected political leader in Islamic history although he had to later contend with many uprisings in his six years tenure. The fifth Caliph *Muawiyah,* whose election is considered controversial by many historians, nominated his son Yazid as his heir. This act established dynastic politics in Muslim *Ummah* which was a departure from the endorsement of a political position through nomination and popular allegiance. Later rulers would use this precedence to nominate their sons as successors.

Islam promotes an idea that ancestry alone does not guarantee piety of a person. An individual has to exhibit personal qualities of righteousness to gain stature in a community. The Quran narrates stories of the father of Prophet Ibrahim (AS) who was an infidel as well as a son of Prophet Noah (AS) who could not be saved from the flood because of his disbelief. Only those individuals that exhibit higher character are considered above others. Islam proposes that when a child is born, he has to embark on the journey of acquiring knowledge and wisdom. The family background of a child may provide access to wealth and a good education, but it is his own performance and character that should dictate his rise in society. It is the best form of social justice and equal rights. Inheritance of wealth and social status of a family do not alone justify qualification for power.

Those who seek political power are advised by the Quran that they will be subjected to a separate judgment for their performance as elected officials. Politicians are advised that they may get away from corruption in this world, but they will face severe punishment for those deeds on the Day of Judgment. Anyone that accepts and assumes political power has to perform soul searching to ascertain that they will be able to discharge his responsibilities with honesty and compassion for the people.

The Chief Executive and his team are custodians of state assets with fiduciary responsibility. Unlike a secular system, in the Islamic social state leaders do not enjoy exemption from prosecution in discharging their responsibilities as elected officials. Civil and criminal cases can be filed against rulers in a court of law and if found guilty they can be punished as per the laws applicable to all other citizens. On the other hand, if an accusation was false then the accuser has to be punished severely to discourage others from petitioning false claims. As long as the executive is in power no one can question the integrity of their intent in executing matters. In an Islamic concept of distribution of power, the Judiciary can reprimand the Amir (President) for abuse of power but cannot remove him from office. The mandate to impeach or recall an executive is granted to the people at large.

The *Amir ul Muluk* (President) is expected to unite the people, uphold justice and maintain equity among citizens rather than serve the narrow interest of a group, ethnicity or sect. Oath of office is not only taken by the elected-Amir but people have to pledge an allegiance to him even those that have voted against him in election. This allegiance to a powerful executive is presented as an authoritarian streak in Islamic concept of government. It is a myth that the Quran mandate absolute power to an Amir. The reality is that the political power of an Amir is balanced by the interplay of three forces. Constitution can limit the executive powers of an Amir by requiring approval of cabinet and judicial nominations by *Majlis-e-shura* as well as declaration of emergencies or ratification of treaties. Declaration of war or an extraordinary increase in budget has to be approved by *Majlis-e-Shura* (Parliament). These provisions in the constitution create limits on executive power. The Amir also does not enjoy immunity from the law. Citizens can file petitions to seek justice in cases of corruption and nepotism. This citizen activism is another limit on unchecked executive authority. Similarly, if an Amir engages in frequent incidents of corruption, injustice or creates a wedge among people then it is required that people should rise up to recall him from office to elect a new executive.

The Amir (President) of an Islamic State is instructed to resort to consultation not only with his cabinet and *Majlis-e-shura* but also with people at large. This concept of consulting with people, introduced 14 centuries ago, is similar to opinion polls conducted by think tanks in Western democracies.

Election Process

Political Parties

(Verse 2.143) *Thus, have We made of you an Ummat justly balanced, that ye might be witnesses over the nations, and the Messenger a witness over yourselves; and We appointed the Qibla to which thou wast used, only to test those who followed the Messenger from those who would turn on their heels (From the Faith). Indeed it was (A change) momentous, except to those guided by Allah. And never would Allah make your faith of no effect. For Allah is to all people most surely full of kindness, Most Merciful.*

(Verse 2.148) *To each is a goal to which Allah turns him; then strive together (as in a race) towards all that is good. Wheresoever ye are, Allah will bring you together. For Allah Hath power over all things.*

(Verse 3.103) *And hold fast, all together, by the rope which Allah (stretches out for you), and be not divided among yourselves; and remember with gratitude Allah's favour on you; for ye were enemies and He joined your hearts in love, so that by His Grace, ye became brethren; and ye were on the brink of the pit of Fire, and He saved you from it. Thus doth Allah make His Signs clear to you: That ye may be guided.* ***(Verse 3.104)*** *Let there arise out of you a band of people inviting to all that is good, enjoining what is right, and forbidding what is wrong: They are the ones to attain felicity.* ***(Verse 3.105)*** *Be not like those who are divided amongst themselves and fall into disputations after receiving Clear Signs: For them is a dreadful penalty,-*

(Verse 6.159) *As for those who divide their religion and break up into sects, thou hast no part in them in the least: their affair is with Allah: He will in the end tell them the truth of all that they did.*

(Verse 9.107) *And there are those who put up a mosque by way of mischief and infidelity - to disunite the Believers - and in preparation for one who warred against Allah and His Messenger aforetime. They will indeed swear that their intention is nothing but good; but Allah doth declare that they are certainly liars.*

(Verse 11.018) *Who doth more wrong than those who invent a lie against Allah? They will be turned back to the presence of their Lord, and the witnesses will say,*

"These are the ones who lied against their Lord! Behold! the Curse of Allah is on those who do wrong!- **(Verse 11.019)** *"Those who would hinder (men) from the path of Allah and would seek in it something crooked: these were they who denied the Hereafter!"*

(Verse 16.116) *But say not - for any false thing that your tongues may put forth,- "This is lawful, and this is forbidden," so as to ascribe false things to Allah. For those who ascribe false things to Allah, will never prosper.*

(Verse 45.017) *And We granted them Clear Signs in affairs (of Religion): it was only after knowledge had been granted to them that they fell into schisms, through insolent envy among themselves. Verily thy Lord will judge between them on the Day of Judgment as to those matters in which they set up differences.*

(Verse 30.032) *Those who split up their Religion, and become (mere) Sects,- each party rejoicing in that which is with itself!*

Divisions or sects based on minor ideological differences are looked down upon in an Islamic Social State. Rather it is expected that the entire community is united in following one ideology presented in the Quran and exemplified by Prophet Mohammad (PBUH). In the secular concept of democracy political parties are formed based on ideological differences in organizing affairs of the community. In America, which is considered one of the most successful experiments in secular democracy, the Republican Party is anti-abortion, against big government and favoring low taxes. While the Democratic Party is pro-choice, in favor of higher taxes and in favor of social services resulting in big government. In an Islamic concept of democracy these ideological differences have no place to carve out the community in different segments. Islamic social entity does not have political parties that divide the community on superficial differences in terms of approach to administration of community. It also does not promote the formation of one dominant political party that controls the affairs of State as in a communist system. Islamic concept of politics looks down upon dynastic monarchy as well. Instead, Islam suggests that the community should elect the best among them to become members of *Majlis-e-shura*, cabinet or Amil-ul-Muluk through a popular vote and an oath of allegiance. Islam promotes a concept that all elected representatives should agree to adhere to the social values (chapter 2) promoted by Islam. Elected representatives can disagree on administrative approach to organizing a society i.e. taxation, wars etc. An advantage of this approach is that candidates do not have to limit themselves to agreeing to a narrow agenda of a political party to contest elections. To seek political mandate or re-election they don't have to appeal to supporters of a political party but to all voters. Voters, on the other hand, choose their representatives based on their qualifications to serve the community rather than affiliation with a political platform.

Another justification presented in favor of organizing political parties is that the process of legislation becomes much more structured. The presence of a small number of political parties, rather than hundreds of individual opinions of independent parliamentarians, makes it possible to have political compromise on policy options. This issue is not relevant because in an Islamic State legislature does not have absolute legislative powers. Instead, they draft legislation through debate and voting in parliament which is then placed on a ballot paper to be ratified by citizens. Constitution can grant parliamentarians the power of approving cabinet nominations of Amir, budgets, treaties, alliances and declaration of war which are operational matters.

In the non-party form of election party manifesto is replaced by social demands of constituents to inform candidates about their expectations once they are elected to office. Some may raise the issue that when candidates are nominated by the community with varying interests then how is it different from a political party? The difference is that the elected candidate, who gets a majority vote, is not bound to just accept one set of interests. To maintain their political mandate, they have to look at all the interests presented by the community and then prioritize it. Some may argue that elected representatives will be obliged to return the favor to the people that nominated them. This is balanced by the fact that if the elected representative is not able to satisfy a majority, then his chances of re-election are reduced. On the other hand, voters have the right to recall a representative, by filing a petition, if he does not meet their expectations. The qualifications for recall should be defined in the constitution and the hurdle should be high enough to avoid abuse by an interest group. For instance, a certain percentage of voters have to sign a petition or a conviction in a criminal/corruption case. In many secular democracies elections for Mayors and City Councils are held on a non-party basis so it is not a totally alien idea. A system can be developed to conduct national and provincial/county elections on a non-party basis.

In a pluralistic society a citizen enjoys multiple associations by joining civic associations, non-profit organizations and industry groups as well as becoming part of commercial organizations to earn a livelihood. Interest groups can be formed to safeguard their particular interests, for instance labor unions, consumer protection associations and trade associations. These associations are not allowed to nominate but they can endorse a candidate during elections.

Nominations of Candidates

Another unique feature of the Islamic concept of election is that candidates cannot present themselves for election but rather people should propose their names. The constitution can outline minimum qualification criteria for a person to contest election. These could include proof of citizenship of the State; minimum years of residency in a constituency; minimum age; being a registered voter; minimum educational qualification; and a clean criminal record and being free from accusation of financial misappropriation. The constitution can lay down a threshold for minimum number of supporters for nomination of candidates to ensure that only people with a significant support base can contest general elections. Nominators of the candidates then run their campaigns to convince the majority of people to vote. This takes the burden off the candidate to make deals with power brokers to win elections. It also removes financial constraints for candidates to seek campaign funds from donors and become obligated to serve their interest if they are elected. In countries where candidates spend their own money to win elections, politics becomes a business rather than a platform to serve.

The objective of Islamic concept of elections is to reduce conflict of interest arising from candidate's advocacy for himself and alignment with political parties with narrower agenda. Islamic concept of democracy is closer to human nature by empowering citizens to have complete freedom to choose their representative not only at the nomination stage but in the general elections as well.

In a similar vein people have the right to recall their representative if they feel they are not fulfilling their commitments or departing from the social values agreed upon by the community. The constitution can lay down the procedure for recall. For example, if an elected representative is convicted of a crime, they lose their membership of the parliament and new elections are held to fill that position. Another incidence could be that a certain percentage of registered voters, in a constituency, submit a written petition to the speaker of *Majlis-e-Shura* (parliament) that they want to recall their member. In that case recalled parliamentarian can contest again to be re-elected but if they are convicted of corruption or a crime, they are disqualified from holding public office.

People should compare qualified candidates when nominating or electing a member of *Majlis-e-shura* based on following criteria:

1. Experience in dealing with public matters as member of non-profit organization, city administration or business management
2. Understand, interpret and formulate laws in the context of public interest
3. Ability to solve social issues
4. Inspire and lead people
5. An unblemished record as upholder of public trust
6. Good reputation as a community member without any criminal or civic convictions

Constitution can lay down minimum conditions for nomination to prevent candidates that do not enjoy wide support. These conditions could include a minimum percentage of registered voters that support the nomination of the candidate; a minimum period of residency in a constituency; no criminal record; and citizenship of the State.

The number and allocation of seats of the legislature, within a State, will depend on the population of districts as well as the diversity of the community. There are many Muslim countries where there is presence of multiple cultural groups and sects. Turkey has a majority of Turkic speaking people but also a significant minority Kurds that are concentrated in certain parts of the country. Similarly in Pakistan there are Sindhi, Balochi, Punjabi, Saraiki, Pashtoon and Urdu speaking communities with their own unique culture. In Malaysia there are significant populations of Malay, Chinese and Tamil people. The formula for allocation of seats among diverse groups should be such that they reflect the underlying composition of the community. Demographics are never static because of varying birth and mortality rates. Formula for seat allocation should incorporate periodic census to adjust any changes in demographics.

Election of the Amir ul Muluk (President) is through a direct non-party vote. The constitution can lay down minimum qualification criteria. These could be that citizens nominating a candidate should come from all provinces or districts of the State. That the person has some experience in public affairs through their management of non-profit charitable organizations or civic interest groups. The person should have no criminal record and should be a citizen of the State.

Islam encourages the community to be active in the affairs of State rather than become passive after casting their vote. This is a substantial difference between popular democracy of a secular state and Islamic Social State.

Legislature

*(**Verse 33.036**) It is not fitting for a Believer, man or woman, when a matter has been decided by Allah and His Messenger to have any option about their decision: if any one disobeys Allah and His Messenger, he is indeed on a clearly wrong Path.*

*(**Verse 35.039**) He it is That has made you inheritors in the earth: if, then, any do reject (Allah), their rejection (works) against themselves: their rejection but adds to the odium for the Unbelievers in the sight of their Lord: their rejection but adds to (their own) undoing.*

(Verse 38.026) *O David! We did indeed make thee a vicegerent on earth: so judge thou between men in truth (and justice): Nor follow thou the lusts (of thy heart), for they will mislead thee from the Path of Allah: for those who wander astray from the Path of Allah, is a Penalty Grievous, for that they forget the Day of Account.*

(Verse 42.038) *Those who hearken to their Lord, and establish regular Prayer; who (conduct) their affairs by mutual Consultation; who spend out of what We bestow on them for Sustenance;*

In many Islamic political science books, the idea is promoted that legislative powers of an assembly are un-Islamic because the Quran and *Sunnah* provides answers to all our temporal problems. As a universal religion for all times to come, it cannot be expected that the understanding of divine message of the Quran is frozen in a by gone era. The Quran repeatedly challenges people to ponder on its message to lead a life of temporal and spiritual salvation. Legislation to manage community affairs are within the free will bestowed on Adam and his progeny by the grace of God. The Quran and *Sunnah* offer a set of values that have to be maintained in all human endeavors but do not restrict creation of a legislative assembly, *Majlis-e-Shura,* to solve social issues arising from an evolving human society. There was no Facebook or twitter 1400 years ago or a YouTube video site that enabled us to interact and collaborate. These services have a significant impact on the social values of a community which have to be incorporated rather than ignored. Laws have to be formulated to regulate these services to ensure that the society benefits from progress in science and technology without damaging the moral fabric presented by Islam. Similarly, women pictures on passports or other identity cards may be anathema to a conservative Muslim but an important tool in managing the social services in a State.

Demographics of a society are dynamic and change over time. Human civilization has evolved from caves to engage in farming and eventually to industrialized urban centers. Tribalism has evolved into a nation state which was initially ruled by a Monarch but later converted to a republic introducing democracy. Issues of each form of society are different and require an evolving social structure to deal with it. It is for this reason the Quran or *Sunnah* did not mandate a particular structure or form of government. It was left to the community and its elected leaders to solve their contemporary issues.

The legislative process is bound by two limiting principles:

1. Each member of community is granted the status of *Khalifa* (vice regent) on earth by God. No law can be enacted that affects the rights of a citizen without conducting a referendum seeking approval of the whole community. An example could be that a legislation that adopts a particular interpretation of Quranic doctrine cannot be adopted unless voted by the whole community.
2. Laws cannot undermine social values promoted by the Quran as outlined in chapter 2. A good example can be that no laws can be made that limits the freedom of religion of citizen which is the right granted to them by God. Or enactment of laws that allow development of monopoly in the marketplace as it will be against the social values presented by the Quran. For instance, legislation banning women driving a car or imposing a condition that they wear a *hijab* is against the Islamic values and hence cannot be approved. Similarly, legislation that allows public consumption of alcohol cannot be approved as well.

The Quran (verse 4.059) advises believers to respect authority and appeal to it to ensure justice and fair play. Legislation relating to granting authority or other administrative purposes has to be done in two steps. *Majlis-e-Shura* has to draft regulations which are then made public for comments that are incorporated after consideration. At the draft stage citizens have the right to file a petition in constitutional courts to stop passage of the bill or seek forced amendments to it.

Judiciary

(Verse 2.188) *And do not eat up your property among yourselves for vanities, nor use it as bait for the judges, with intent that ye may eat up wrongfully and knowingly a little of (other) people's property.*

(Verse 3.018) *There is no god but He: That is the witness of Allah, His angels, and those endued with knowledge, standing firm on justice. There is no god but He, the Exalted in Power, the Wise.*

(Verse 4.058) *Allah doth command you to render back your Trusts to those to whom they are due; And when ye judge between man and man, that ye judge with justice: Verily how excellent is the teaching which He giveth you! For Allah is He Who heareth and seeth all things.*

(Verse 4.105) *We have sent down to thee the Book in truth, that thou mightest judge between men, as guided by Allah: so be not (used) as an advocate by those who betray their trust;*

(Verse 5.042) *(They are fond of) listening to falsehood, of devouring anything forbidden. If they do come to thee, either judge between them, or decline to interfere. If thou decline, they cannot hurt thee in the least. If thou judge, judge in equity between them. For Allah loveth those who judge in equity.*

(Verse 5.045) *We ordained therein for them: "Life for life, eye for eye, nose or nose, ear for ear, tooth for tooth, and wounds equal for equal." But if any one remits the retaliation by way of charity, it is an act of atonement for himself. And if any fail to judge by (the light of) what Allah hath revealed, they are (No better than) wrong-doers.*

(Verse 35.018) *Nor can a bearer of burdens bear another's burdens if one heavily laden should call another to (bear) his load. Not the least portion of it can be carried (by the other). Even though he be nearly related. Thou canst but admonish such as fear their Lord unseen and establish regular Prayer. And whoever purifies himself does so for the benefit of his own soul; and the destination (of all) is to Allah.*

(Verse 42.040) *The recompense for an injury is an injury equal thereto (in degree): but if a person forgives and makes reconciliation, his reward is due from Allah: for (Allah) loveth not those who do wrong.* ***(Verse 42.041)*** *But indeed if any do help and defend themselves after a wrong (done) to them, against such there is* *no cause of blame.* **(Verse 42.042)** *The blame is only against those who oppress men and wrong-doing and insolently transgress beyond bounds through the land, defying right and justice: for such there will be a penalty grievous.* **(Verse 53.038)** *Namely, that no bearer of burdens can bear the burden of another;*

Article from Charter of Medinah:

(21) Whoever is convicted of killing a believer without good reason shall be subject to retaliation unless the next of kin is satisfied (with blood-money), and the believers shall be against him as one man, and they are bound to take action against him.

In an Islamic State the Judiciary is one of the most important functions of government and considered the foundation stone for the survival of a community as a State. Judiciary should be independent from interference from executive and legislative branches of the government. No one in an Islamic state is beyond the reach of justice even the Amir-ul-Muluk (President), who holds the highest office in the State. These powers are evident from the Quranic verses, *Sunnah* (tradition) of the Prophet and historical records of rightly guided Caliphs. Nomination of *Qadis* (judges) is the prerogative of the Amir. To create balance of power and include will of the people, who are the ultimate sovereign, constitution may require approval by *Majlis-e-Shura* (parliament) of *Qadis* nominated by the Amir. Once *Qadis* are appointment they operate independently to review cases based on the penal code and constitution. People have the right to file complaints against *Qadis* that engage in a bias when awarding judgments or engage in acceptance of bribes. Erosion of credibility of a *Qadi* can become cause for their replaced. To provide protection, the constitution may impede executive or legislative branches from removing a *Qadi*. This right can be either granted to the people when a certain percentage of registered voters file a petition to seek replacement, or an Amir may seek approval of the people to replace a *Qadi* by placing this question on a ballot paper during the election process. Another reason for replacement could be if a *Qadi* is proved to have accepted bribes, in which case, Amir could submit request for removal of a *Qadi* to a *Majlis-e-Shura* along with nomination of a replacement.

Citizens who meet following criteria can be considered for nomination as *Qadis*:

1. Unblemished reputation as upholder and practitioners of law and ethics.
2. Substantial experience of practicing law
3. Citizen of the State

The system of justice operates under supervision and guidance of the Chief *Qadi* (chief justice). Chief *Qadi* has to ensure that judicial benches are easily and conveniently available throughout the State. He/she can create separate benches for constitutional, criminal, civil and family cases to expedite cases and prevent delays. The State has to provide sufficient resources to establish a speedy and affordable justice system without discrimination against any one segment of the community. A Chief *Qadi* that is not able to ensure timely and fair judgments to the citizens can be replaced by the Amir as per the procedure outlined in the constitution. *Qadis* are subjected to public scrutiny through the quality of their judgments and personal conduct. Frequent complaints from people about verdicts of a *Qadi* will require inquiry by the Chief *Qadi* to either prove his innocence or advise replacement.

Islam promotes that a convict is innocent until proven guilty. Anyone that engages in false accusations of innocent citizens is barred from holding public office, life ban on providing evidence and severely punished for repeated offense. The Law of Evidence must conform to the privacy, basic rights and social values incorporated in the constitution. Citizens are expected to voluntarily come forward to provide evidence against convicts that are guilty but also to help release those that are wrongfully accused.

The Islamic system of justice is based on the following principles:

1. No one is above the law including the head of the government. Some may argue that cases against the head of government could distract them from functioning effectively or that it could limit executive authority. Powers of courts are limited to punishing for a particular crime that might have been committed by the head of government. They don't have the power to remove them from office as it is the right granted to the people by the constitution.
2. All citizens are expected to help the judiciary by voluntarily providing

evidence without waiting to be subpoenaed by the court. Failure to provide evidence or falsifying it could be considered a breach of social contract and might be punishable by a civil penalty.

3. Establishing a just society is the responsibility of all citizens. Islam encourages wealthy individuals to sponsor legal-aid organizations to help those who cannot afford it. The State can help these organizations by providing them with financial support. It is the responsibility of society at large to provide a fair trial to all accused.
4. Crimes are not considered against the State or community if the affected party is known, or the criminal has acted once with a personal motive. In these cases, the State cannot become party to the judgment and seek reprisal for the act from the court. Islam grants the affected party the right to have a voice in imposing a penalty on the criminal. For instance, in the case of non-premeditated murder, the guilty party can offer compensation in return for clemency. While in case of a premeditated murder it has an element of crime against society which allows the State to seek a penalty as well, apart from the compensation offered to the affected party. But in that case if an affected party foregoes capital punishment, then the prosecutor cannot seek it. Similarly in the case of theft, a repeat offender is considered a danger to society and may have to be punished by amputation as prescribed in the Quran as well as paying compensation to the affected party.
5. In an Islamic State the final appeal can be made to the office of Amir ul Muluk (President) in cases of capital punishment. It is then the right of the Amir to send it for retrial or uphold the verdict of the court.
6. Islam does not support dual or multiple judicial systems that can contradict each other or overlap in authority. There has to be one system of justice throughout the state which is administered by the judiciary. In a federation there cannot be a dual system of State/provincial and a federal justice system. The state forms one community while counties/provinces are just an administrative arrangement with no legal authority of their own.

Islam allows provision for due process, but it should not be so cumbersome that it delays the justice or increases the cost prohibitively. At the start of each case the judge can lay down the procedure to be adopted for the case based on its unique characteristics to which both prosecutor and defendant have to agree to. This procedure has to ensure that sufficient time is provided to the defendant to plead their case without delaying the justice unnecessarily. Minor crimes, small claims or misdemeanor charges should be decided in one hearing. Islamic Social values promotes expectations that each party involved in the case will adhere to the value of justice i.e. to be truthful to stop injustice. For instance, in case of tax evasion the real charge is lying to the community about income. In that case tax officials, after seeking approval from the court, have to inform the local community and seek their help to become respondents against the evader. The idea is that the State in itself has no interest of its own; rather it is the repository of interest of individual citizens. It is the responsibility of citizens to take active interest in holding each other accountable for their social behavior.

In a diverse society where citizens of different faiths are involved in a case, a *Qadi* must seek expert advice from religious scholars to understand their moral and ethical position especially related to partnerships, family matters and inheritance.

Islamic Penal Code

Sharia literally means way of life. *Sharia,* developed by scholars, provides guidance to ensure adherence to the moral social code adopted in the constitution. In recent times general understanding of *Sharia* is more narrowly defined as the Islamic penal code. *Fiqh* is a more appropriate term that relates to Islamic legal code. Many Muslims, mistakenly, equate this legal code at par with revelation from God and consider it immutable. Islamic *Fiqh* was developed by Muslim jurists during the first few centuries of the advent of Islam. It is the legal codification of values and ethics presented in the Quran and *Sunnah.* Unfortunately, development of this legal code was neglected after the Abbasid era. This has severely limited the contemporary applicability of this important instrument of the Islamic Social Contract. After gaining independence, majority of Muslim countries have retained the Western penal code that was in force during the time of their occupation. It is interesting that many features of the Western penal code are borrowed from Islamic *Fiqh*. Provision of legal aid to convicts and presumption of innocence unless proven guilty were practiced in Muslim lands before they were introduced to the Western civilization around 17th century. The concept of neutrality of justice is another value derived from Islam. This value was part of the Charter of Medinah (Appendix I) when all tribes that were party to it agreed that a convict would not be granted tribal protection. It is imperative that research is re initiated, in Muslim majority countries, to develop a well-structured penal code that can meet the needs of contemporary times.

The objective of any law is to empower the State with coercive power that becomes a psychological barrier to prevent citizens to engage in crimes. A State that is not able to exercise this power or becomes unfair in exercising it eventually dissipates into civil unrest and anarchy. There is no society in the world that does not have a police force. It is recognition of the human condition that it is not possible to completely eradicate crime from society. In every community there are some members that have the potential to cross a barrier and commit crimes against other members. Motivation for crimes is either the result of social injustice in a society or driven by emotions of envy, greed and revenge. The Islamic concept of justice suggests that practicing social justice is the best prevention while a penal code is a last resort to protect the lives, liberties and property of citizens.

A legal code should not be static but rather evolve over time as advances are made in social organization. To facilitate this social evolution, Muslim jurists have to remain engaged in *ijma*(consensus), *qiyas* (analogy) and *ijtihad* (independent reasoning) at all times. At no point, in social development should it be considered that development of an Islamic penal code is complete. The law must be able to deal with contemporary issues utilizing the tools made available from advancement in sciences. DNA and genetic engineering can raise issues related to bioethics or intellectual property issues arising from innovations. To develop a universal Islamic panel code the Organization of Islamic Cooperation (OIC), Gulf Cooperation Council (GCC) and other platforms should form committees to work on this important community building tool that can advance implementation of an Islamic Social contract.

The Quran deals with issues that are more personal in nature, for instance it offers guidance in dealing with divorce, marriage, adultery, adoption of children and distribution of inheritance.

(Verse 4.015) *If any of your women are guilty of lewdness, take the evidence of four (Reliable) witnesses from amongst you against them; and if they testify, confine them to houses until death do claim them, or Allah ordain for them some (other) way.*

(Verse 4.016) *If two men among you are guilty of lewdness, punish them both. If they repent and amend, leave them alone; for Allah is Oft-returning, Most Merciful.*

(Verse 24.002) *The woman and the man guilty of adultery or fornication,- flog each of them with a hundred stripes: Let not compassion move you in their case, in a matter prescribed by Allah, if ye believe in Allah and the Last Day: and let a party of the Believers witness their punishment. (Verse 24.003) Let no man guilty of adultery or fornication marry and but a woman similarly guilty, or an Unbeliever: nor let any but such a man or an Unbeliever marry such a woman: to the Believers such a thing is forbidden.*

There are many issues that require deeper investigation when considering adjudication of crimes such as theft. There is a common belief among people that the Islamic penal code prescribes amputation of limbs of all convicted thieves. This question has been discussed by many Muslim jurists. A thief that is unemployed, is a first-time offender or is subjected to oppression by society is treated differently from a person that commits repeat offense.

(Verse 5.038) *As to the thief, Male or female, cut off his or her hands: a punishment by way of example, from Allah, for their crime: and Allah is Exalted in power.* ***(Verse 5.039)*** *But if the thief repents after his crime, and amends his conduct, Allah turneth to him in forgiveness; for Allah is Oft-forgiving, Most Merciful.*

Verse 5.039 makes it clear that first time offenders can be given lighter corrective sentences, if they repent and promise to amend their conduct. This value is adopted by the Western penal code in which first time offenders are punished lightly by requiring them to work in community service, without compensation, while serial offenders are treated harshly. Secondly, the scope of theft is also considered. If someone is stealing high value items, he is treated differently as compared to those who stole food under duress. In contemporary times theft is not related to physical goods alone. Intellectual property, stealing debit cards, and sales of digital goods have introduced new forms of theft. These require research from Islamic jurists to incorporate it into the penal code.

Punishment for adultery is another widely debated crime in Muslim societies. Secularists blame Muslims to have a bias against women in dealing with cases of adultery. The way Muslim societies approach these cases may justify their claims. Here are some verses of the Quran dealing with this issue:

*(**Verse 24.002**) The woman and the man guilty of adultery or fornication,- flog each of them with a hundred stripes: Let not compassion move you in their case, in a matter prescribed by Allah, if ye believe in Allah and the Last Day: and let a party of the Believers witness their punishment. (**Verse 24.003**) Let no man guilty of adultery or fornication marry and but a woman similarly guilty, or an Unbeliever: nor let any but such a man or an Unbeliever marry such a woman: to the Believers such a thing is forbidden.*

These verses make it quite clear that punishment for adultery is both corporal and social. Corporal punishment is 100 stripes in public which is humiliating to the convict. The second part is a social reprimand when it is instructed that men or women convicted of adultery can only marry those that are convicted in a similar crime. Nowhere in the Quran is it mentioned that convicts should be stoned to death. Some legal scholars justify that punishment by stoning is based on certain *hadith* from the tradition of Prophet Mohammad (PBUH). Some historians, on the other hand, claim that the first incidence of severe punishment for adultery was during the time of Caliph Umar. Conditions of providing evidence for adultery are very strict which are neglected in majority of Muslim countries when dealing with these kinds of cases. It is important that research is done on this issue because the life of Prophet Mohammad (PBUH) reflects the Quran and cannot contradict its teachings.

To protect women against false charges the Quran makes it clear that anyone engaged in false accusation, women particularly and men generally, has to be punished in the similar manner.

(Verse 24.004) *And those who launch a charge against chaste women, and produce not four witnesses (to support their allegations),- flog them with eighty stripes; and reject their evidence ever after: for such men are wicked transgressors;-*

(Verse 24.012) *Why did not the believers - men and women - when ye heard of the affair,- put the best construction on it in their own minds and say, "This (charge) is an obvious lie"?* ***(Verse 24.013)*** *Why did they not bring four witnesses to prove it? When they have not brought the witnesses, such men, in the sight of Allah, (stand forth) themselves as liars!* ***(Verse 24.014)*** *Were it not for the grace and mercy of Allah on you, in this world and the Hereafter, a grievous penalty would have seized you in that ye rushed glibly into this affair.*

Unfortunately, in many Muslims countries false accusers are rarely punished for their crimes. In verses 24.012-014 God instructs that those who maintain silence when a false charge is brought against women will be punished acutely in the afterlife.

Similar discrepancies exist in almost all parts of the *Fiqh* (Islamic legal code) that require clarification through research and codification. Selective interpretation of the Islamic penal code and lack of new research has created more damage than good. It is important that Muslims develop and refine their legal code so that it can become part of the Universal justice system.

Another thing to consider is the application of multiple codes in a society. During Ottoman times there were three different codes in practice simultaneously. These included *Qanun* (laws) related to administration of the state handled by *Mazalim* (injustice) courts. *Sharia* (family law) code was implemented by *Sharia* courts, staffed by *Ulema*. And finally, *Millat* (nation) code dealing with cases of non-Muslims. Implementation of Western legal codes in large number of countries have demonstrated that a universal code can be effectively applied. Islamic *Fiqh* that evolves after incorporating contemporary social conditions can be more adaptable for Muslim majority countries and can add to development of stable societies. To deal with non-Muslim cases, related to divorce, inheritance and child adoption, *Qadis* can call upon experts of that particular religion before issuing a verdict. Punishment for criminal cases, for instance amputation of limbs of a serial thief, is secular in nature because the objective is to create a psychological barrier. A Muslims or non-Muslim, regardless of their religion, should refrain from stealing if they want to save their limb.

Another issue that has to be tackled is the indiscriminate issuance of *fatwas* (legal edicts) by *Ulema* (religious scholars). This is a source of confusion because doctrinal differences prevail among various schools of Islamic jurisprudence including Shafi, Hanbali, Hanifi, Maliki to name just few. There are also regional schools of thought. For instance, in South Asia there are Deobandi and Barelvi schools. Issuance of *fatwas* also impinges on the authority of State to implement a unified penal code and in many instances becomes cause for anarchy and social unrest. This practice has to be regularized so that input of the *Ulema* is incorporated by the jurists at the time of developing a code. Once this code is promulgated it has to be accepted by all schools and sects. Islam promotes the idea of reducing differences and creating a cohesive community. Any sect that refuses to accept the penal code adopted by the State abrogates the social contract. If they try to violate the law and create danger to peace, the State should use full force of law against them. During the time of the first Caliph *Abu Bakr* a segment of the community tried to redefine the concept of *zakat* and refused to pay it. Caliph *Abu Bakr* waged a full-scale war to defeat those dissenters even when companions of the prophet advised him to try to compromise with them. Similarly, when Caliph Ali signed a peace treaty with Governor of Syria *Muawiyah,* after the war of Siffin, a segment of the community later called *kharjites,* refused to accept it. Caliph Ali initiated a campaign until the majority of them were brought under State control.

Government Functionaries

In an Islamic Social State, the hiring of government officials is based on merit and capability without any consideration of social, ethnic and religious affiliations of a person. The diversity of government officials should mirror the underlying community. Absence of social balance in hiring of officials would in a way indicate that social justice is not prevalent. In a just society all segments of society should be able to offer a sufficient number of recruits for government positions. When Muslims conquered Sindh, Iraq and Iran they ensured that social justice is practiced in managing the affairs of the State. Islamic values of justice and fair play encouraged participation from conquered people reducing chances of retaliation. In many cases people welcomed their new rulers.

In discharging their duties, it is expected that government officials will act as custodian of public trust and not engage in corruption. The Quran makes it clear that officials holding public trust will be judged on the Day of Judgment about their honesty in managing these affairs. There are many stories from the first four caliphs when people questioned them about misappropriating public treasury and they had to defend their innocence.

Citizens of the Islamic Social State are expected to keep an eye on performance of public officials and raise their voice when they witness misappropriation and misconduct. Appraisal of government officials should include the opinion of people so that only those rises in ranks that are honest and are able to maintain public trust. In return for their services, the State has to ensure that officials are adequately compensated to lead a comfortable lifestyle. The size of the State machinery should be adequate to discharge the responsibilities without burdening the community. Extraordinary expansion of State employment or expansion of government role has to be subjected to approval from *Majlis-eShura* as it is the community that ultimately bears the cost of it.

Islamic Economy

Social justice in its tangible form manifests in fair distribution of economic opportunity without discriminating based on ethnicity and sectarian affiliation. A social contract without an accompanying economic order cannot exist in reality. An important component of an Islamic economic system is creating a level playing field by reducing barriers to entry, recognizing private property and equitable contribution towards State exchequer. Islam recognizes that engaging in a career to earn livelihood is intrinsic to human condition and one of the reasons for social association. Islam proposes a capitalist system in which there is no restriction imposed on the flow of capital, goods and services as long as social values are preserved. A State, in an Islamic economic model, cannot impose protectionist tariff or impose a visa regime that restricts free flow of labor. The treaties signed with other States should reflect these values.

In an Islamic state the government cannot own a commercial enterprise to compete with her citizens for profit. The objective of the government is to regulate economic activity of citizens to ensure that they do not abrogate rights of others in their persuasion of gains. Economic model of an Islamic state depends on upholding following values:

1. Ensure that citizens have equal access to economic opportunities.
2. Maintain a balanced budget to avoid surplus or deficit.
3. State cannot compete with her citizens in the marketplace.
4. Recognition that capabilities of citizens are not uniform. Citizens that are successful cannot be penalized for it.

5. The state has to prosecute those that engage in unethical practices in wealth creation.
6. Private property rights of citizens should be respected and protected
7. Citizens have to be active participants in the provision of social services in their communities. State has to regulate non-profit organizations and provide support in case of a deficit.

Economic Equality

*(**Verse 2.219**) They ask thee concerning wine and gambling. Say: "In them is great sin, and some profit, for men; but the sin is greater than the profit." They ask thee how much they are to spend; Say: "What is beyond your needs." Thus doth Allah Make clear to you His Signs: In order that ye may consider-*

*(**Verse 3.134**) Those who spend (freely), whether in prosperity, or in adversity; who restrain anger, and pardon (all) men;- for Allah loves those who do good;-*

*(**Verse 51.019**) And in their wealth and possessions (was remembered) the right of the (needy,) him who asked, and him who (for some reason) was prevented (from asking).*

Islamic Social State can achieve economic equality by instituting following measures in a community:

1. A fair system of compensation
2. Encourage profit sharing between owners and their labor teams
3. Voluntary contribution by wealthy individuals to invest their surplus income in small enterprises through equity participation. Spend a portion of their wealth on the creation of non-profit organizations to provide social services in their local communities.
4. State intervention to prevent the formation of cartels, oligarchs, and monopolies so as to prevent unnatural rises in commodity prices. These phenomena could have an adverse effect on the disposable incomes of people which can cause poverty and exacerbate income inequality.
5. State intervention to prevent commodity hoarding and price gouging in times of crisis. The State has to monitor supply and demand conditions

to avoid artificial shortages of commodities with the motive to make higher profit. In the events of natural disasters these can have a sever effect on the purchasing power of people. This is prohibited in the Islamic social system and severely punishable by law.

6. Voluntary effort by sellers to have fair pricing of products. Making an exorbitant profit is considered a socially irresponsible act and one of the causes for economic imbalance. In a purely capitalistic system, the percentage of profit is determined by the supply and demand dynamics of the market. In Islamic social system businesses are not just economic enterprises concerned with profit alone. They also have a social role in terms of creating employment and serving the needs of their customers while making profit in the process. Fair pricing means they have to charge a price that ensures continued existence of the business without undermining social values. The State cannot dictate price but encourages sufficient competition to enable reasonable profitability of market participants.

Social Security

(Verse 2.215) *They ask thee what they should spend (In charity). Say: Whatever ye spend that is good, is for parents and kindred and orphans and those in want and for wayfarers. And whatever ye do that is good, -Allah knoweth it well.*

(Verse 2.273) *(Charity is) for those in need, who, in Allah's cause are restricted (from travel), and cannot move about in the land, seeking (For trade or work): the ignorant man thinks, because of their modesty, that they are free from want. Thou shalt know them by their (Unfailing) mark: They beg not importunately from all the sundry. And whatever of good ye give, be assured Allah knoweth it well.*

(Verse 4.036) *Serve Allah, and join not any partners with Him; and do good- to parents, kinsfolk, orphans, those in need, neighbors who are near, neighbors who are strangers, the companion by your side, the wayfarer (ye meet), and what your right hands possess: For Allah loveth not the arrogant, the vainglorious;-*

(Verse 9.060) *Alms are for the poor and the needy, and those employed to administer the (funds); for those whose hearts have been (recently) reconciled (to*

Truth); for those in bondage and in debt; in the cause of Allah; and for the wayfarer: (thus is it) ordained by Allah, and Allah is full of knowledge and wisdom.

In an Islamic economic system social security is the responsibility of local community at neighborhood level. This system of support is funded by contributions from community members and donations from wealthy individuals. Citizens create non-profit organizations which levies a membership fee on all residents in its mandated area. These social security organizations provide unemployment benefits to its members during periods of lay off and job search. The charter of these corporations can include provision of re-training for people that have a disability and help them find suitable jobs. These organizations can reach out to the corporate sector and wealthy individuals that are willing to offer employment in individual cases.

To alleviate financial loss resulting from unforeseen calamities like car accidents, floods, fires, hospital stays etc. separate neighborhood associations can be created supported through membership fees and charitable donations. These organizations can also provide support to families that need help with hospice care of their old parents. These organizations may also consider providing support to children of low-income families, for higher education through grants and scholarships. These organizations can maintain contacts with networks of wealthy individuals in their areas to refer cases to them for help that comes through their offices.

In case people migrate within the State they can carry over a portion of their membership contributions to their new neighborhood organizations.

Corporations can mitigate their risk of accidental loss by setting aside a reserve to cover those losses or form cooperatives to distribute risks among its members. Accidental losses, although devastating, are not a usual occurrence but rather an unusual event with low probability of a recurrence. It is because of this mathematical reason insurance companies can develop business models and remain profitable. High profitability of insurance companies, despite substantial human resource cost, is an indication that premium paid by insurance holders is much higher than the claims paid out. It is this concept of making profit from misery of people that is against social values of Islam. Islam instructs that taking care of each other is a shared responsibility and is a form of submission to the will of God. A calamity of a member is a test for the whole community while having faith that it is from God. This concept of bearing a loss with perseverance is expressed in the following verse:

(Verse 2.156) *Who say, when afflicted with calamity: "To Allah We belong, and to Him is our return":-*

It should be noted that in Islam there is no concept of retirement which means that a person is expected to work all their lives if they are bodily and mentally healthy. As citizens attain old age their responsibilities will be according to their age and physical strength. Children and grandchildren are responsible for taking care of their old parents and grandparents.

(Verse 17.023) *Thy Lord hath decreed that ye worship none but Him, and that ye be kind to parents. Whether one or both of them attain old age in thy life, say not to them a word of contempt, nor repel them, but address them in terms of honor.* ***(Verse 17.024)*** *And, out of kindness, lower to them the wing of humility, and say: "My Lord! bestow on them thy Mercy even as they cherished me in childhood."*

(Verse 31.014) *And We have enjoined on man (to be good) to his parents: in travail upon travail did his mother bear him, and in years twain was his weaning: (hear the command), "Show gratitude to Me and to thy parents: to Me is (thy final) Goal.*

(Verse 46.015) *We have enjoined on man kindness to his parents: In pain did his mother bear him, and in pain did she give him birth. The carrying of the (child) to his weaning is (a period of) thirty months. At length, when he reaches the age of full strength and attains forty years, he says, "O my Lord! Grant me that I may be grateful for Thy favor which Thou has bestowed upon me, and upon both my parents, and that I may work righteousness such as Thou mayest approve; and be gracious to me in my issue. Truly have I turned to Thee and truly do I bow (to Thee) in Islam."*

A family that may not be able to support their old parents in terms of hospice and any other care can seek help from local social security and *zakat* organizations. The Quran warns children not to neglect their old parents by admitting them into retirement homes and leaving them at the mercy of others.

State Revenue & Taxation

State has to have a balanced budget and is required not to incur budget deficits. Tax rates imposed by the government will depend on the budget projections of the State. This makes tax rates flexible rather than fixed year after year. Changing tax rates on an annual basis keeps the population concerned and engaged rather than become callous when they remain fixed. Prohibition of interest prevents the State from borrowing funds to cover its budget deficit. By transferring social responsibility to citizens, Islam prefers keeping the size of government small, by limiting its role to regulation, refereeing and national security. Small government keeps the budgets low resulting in low tax rates allowing citizens to have higher disposable incomes. City governments can collect property and land taxes to fund their operations.

There is a strong emphasis in Islam that local communities should take an active part in managing services and infrastructure. It encourages the creation of community non-profit private enterprises to provide services like sewage, water, and garbage collection. In developed countries experience has shown that private enterprises are more efficient in resource usage than a public entity which has propensity for wastage, inefficiency and corruption. The State can build large infrastructure projects like major highways and dams that cross provincial/county lines using the concept of build own, operate and transfer (BOT). After completion management of these projects can be transferred to an enterprise that is owned by the local community or a private enterprise depending on the nature of the project. Corporations that get management rights pay a fee until the capital is recovered by the State. The State continues monitoring the companies to ensure that services are delivered as promised. For example, a dam is built by the government and shifted to a private entity for operations and maintenance. A major highway is shifted in portion to local communities for upkeep. Tolls can be imposed by local highway operators to pay back the construction cost incurred by the federal government.

Islam encourages free flow of capital, labor and merchandise across national borders. Protectionist laws and visa regimes are against economic values promoted by Islam. The State can levy tariffs on imported merchandise to provide safety and security for its transit within its borders. In a similar fashion local government can impose a toll for use of port facilities, road network and warehousing of merchants.

Interest (Usury)

*(**Verse 2.275**) Those who devour usury will not stand except as stand one whom the Evil one by his touch Hath driven to madness. That is because they say: "Trade is like usury," but Allah hath permitted trade and forbidden usury. Those who after receiving direction from their Lord, desist, shall be pardoned for the past; their case is for Allah (to judge); but those who repeat (The offence) are companions of the Fire: They will abide therein (for ever). (**Verse 2.276**) Allah will deprive usury of all blessing, but will give increase for deeds of charity: For He loveth not creatures ungrateful and wicked.*

*(**Verse 2.278**) O ye who believe! Fear Allah, and give up what remains of your demand for usury, if ye are indeed believers. (**Verse 2.279**) If ye do it not, Take notice of war from Allah and His Messenger: But if ye turn back, ye shall have your capital sums: Deal not unjustly, and ye shall not be dealt with unjustly. (**Verse 2.280**) If the debtor is in a difficulty, grant him time Till it is easy for him to repay. But if ye remit it by way of charity, that is best for you if ye only knew.*

*(**Verse 3.130**) O ye who believe! Devour not usury, doubled and multiplied; but fear Allah; that ye may (really) prosper.*

*(**Verse 4.161**) That they took usury, though they were forbidden; and that they devoured men's substance wrongfully;- we have prepared for those among them who reject faith a grievous punishment.*

Quote from last sermon of Prophet Mohammad (PBUH):

"ALLAH has forbidden you to take usury (interest), therefore all interest obligation shall henceforth be waived. Your capital, however, is yours to keep. You will neither inflict nor suffer any inequity. Allah has Judged that there shall be no interest and that all the interest due to Abbas ibn 'Abd'al Muttalib (Prophet's uncle) shall henceforth be waived."

In an Islamic economic concept interest has been classified as a social evil and strictly prohibited in any form. Emphasis of Islam is that income should be derived from an active participation in an economic activity rather than earned through a passive mode like interest. Some scholars argue that interest is only prohibited when money is lent to individuals in a transaction between private parties. They justify that it is permitted that institutional lenders i.e. banks and other financial institutions can charge interest. This is a mistaken notion; Islam considers interests an instrument of exploitation and promoter of economic and social divide in the community. Islam labels interest as a source of an emergence of a class-based society in which rich reaps benefits without being active participant in a society. Economists suggest that the social crisis emanating from recession in the West, that has championed modern interest-based banking, can be blamed on multiple layers of interest-based loan derivatives. In this practice banks' lending money to home buyers at a fixed rate of interest then securitizes its portfolio to raise capital while still earning a percentage of interest on the original loan. This concept of leveraging money means that a single dollar can be loaned multiple times. This artificially inflates the stored value of money that endangers the underlying social structure. The whole edifice of modern financial engineering cannot be possible in the absence of interest.

The other issue with interest-based banking is that, from an Islamic perspective, a bank is a custodian of deposits rather than an owner to use it at their discretion. In an Islamic concept of trust a bank cannot lend to another entity unless it gets approval from the depositor to use those funds and informing them about the nature of loan.

Many financial experts argue that the banking industry cannot survive in the absence of interest income. This also raises questions about nature of banking in an Islamic economic system that prohibits interest. Islamic concept of banking depends on the value of mutual trust. In this concept a bank is a service rather than a manufacturing organization which uses money as a raw material to create products using interest-based leveraging. On the other hand, as a service provider, banks can charge fees for their various services to be a profitable enterprise without earning a fixed income on money entrusted to them. In America banks generate a significant portion of their revenue from service fees rather than interest earned on deposits. For instance, when a bank customer makes a cash deposit, they charge a fee of US$1 per 1000 dollars deposited. Similar fees are applied for processing deposits, incoming/outgoing wire transfers, security deposits, issuing bank draft, monthly account maintenance fees, debit card fee etc. Advancements in technology have made it possible for banks to profitably operate on a fee-based model.

Depositors are either interested in banking service for convenience of their business transactions or seek return on their savings. To earn money on deposits Banks can engage in venture financing where they become active participants in a private enterprise. For small depositors banks can own shares in private enterprises on their behalf while for large depositors they can provide active monitoring of investment for a fee. These services can include representation on the board of directors, quarterly audit of the investment and generating market/product research reports for their clients. Banks can also arrange the selling of these private holdings if a depositor wants to exit from an investment. We should remember that Islamic concept of banking is a local enterprise. The bank branch manager is a community member and knows their depositors and neighboring enterprise owners. As a financial expert he is expected to be a person of good business acumen to judge an investment idea on its merit and then propose it to his/her depositors. In a way he/she plays the role of a mediator and charges a fee for service. To achieve economies of scale these branches can combine into a network to form a national bank.

Banks can also help their depositors make profit by engaging in retail finance through no-interest purchasing of merchandise. In this concept profit of a merchandise sold is shared between seller and financier while a consumer gets a chance to pay the retail price in installments over a fixed period of time. For instance, a refrigerator is priced at 10000 earning 15% profit for the merchant. A buyer needs help in buying this product. Bank can provide money to facilitate the purchase which has to be paid by the buyer in 12, 18 or 24 installments. For its service bank lender and seller split the profit on the merchandise equally, that is 7.5% each. Again, it has to be a local bank that knows the merchant and ascertains the financial condition of the buyer to mitigate any risk of non-payment. The bank manager has to consider the credibility of the buyer as well as ensure that they have the capacity to pay the amount without putting strain on their quality of life. Borrowers also have a social responsibility to ensure that they live within their financial resources and should not make purchases that are beyond their means.

In trade finance banks can charge a service fee for providing letters of credit and other instruments. Some may argue that in an interconnected world it is important that interest is incorporated in a banking system. This is another myth that has no basis because like freedom of religion, an Islamic state does not have to impose its requirement of no-interest system on banks that are outside its jurisdiction. Banks that operates within an Islamic State has to conform to local banking regulations. Secondly inter bank transactions can be settled without engaging in interest. When banks interact with each other to settle transactions then usually either money is flowing in or going out and does not necessarily involve interest. It is when an asset or a business is jointly shared by two banks that one of them may require a fixed return on assets. In the initial stage of development that might be a necessary compromise, but once Islamic concept of banking emerge among Muslim majority countries, they should have substantial clout to devise new instruments that do not require any involvement of interest.

Advancement in communication and data storage technologies has substantially reduced the cost of transactions for banks. In contemporary times it is possible to develop financial institutions that are based on the service provider model without relying on interest income. Muslim bankers have to think out of the box to develop successful business models to create interest free banks. Islam prohibits interest and considers it one of a necessary condition to evolve a socially just society.

Business Transactions & Contracts

(Verse 2.282) *O ye who believe! When ye deal with each other, in transactions involving future obligations in a fixed period of time, reduce them to writing Let a scribe write down faithfully as between the parties: let not the scribe refuse to write: as Allah Has taught him, so let him write. Let him who incurs the liability dictate, but let him fear His Lord Allah, and not diminish aught of what he owes. If they party liable is mentally deficient, or weak, or unable Himself to dictate, Let his guardian dictate faithfully, and get two witnesses, out of your own men, and if there are not two men, then a man and two women, such as ye choose, for witnesses, so that if one of them errs, the other can remind her. The witnesses should not refuse when they are called on (For evidence). Disdain not to reduce to writing (your contract) for a future period, whether it be small or big: it is juster in the sight of Allah, More suitable as evidence, and more convenient to prevent doubts among yourselves but if it be a transaction which ye carry out on the spot among yourselves, there is no blame on you if ye reduce it not to writing. But take witness whenever ye make a commercial contract; and let neither scribe nor witness suffer harm. If ye do (such harm), it would be wickedness in you. So fear Allah; For it is Good that teaches you. And Allah is well acquainted with all things. If ye are on a journey, and cannot find a scribe, a pledge with possession (may serve the purpose). And if one of you deposits a thing on trust with another, let the trustee (faithfully) discharge his trust, and let him Fear his Lord conceal not evidence; for whoever conceals it, - his heart is tainted with sin. And Allah knoweth all that ye do.*

(Verse 17.035) *Give full measure when ye measure, and weigh with a balance that is straight: that is the most fitting and the most advantageous in the final determination.*

(Verse 26.181) *"Give just measure, and cause no loss (to others by fraud).* ***(Verse 26.182)*** *"And weigh with scales true and upright.* ***(Verse 26.183)*** *"And withhold not things justly due to men, nor do evil in the land, working mischief.*

(Verse 55.009) *So establish weight with justice and fall not short in the balance.*

(Verse 83.001) *Woe to those that deal in fraud,-* ***(Verse 83.002)*** *Those who, when they have to receive by measure from men, exact full measure,* ***(Verse 83.003)*** *But when they have to give by measure or weight to men, give less than due.*

Business transactions have to be based on mutual trust, but the Quran instructs written agreements are better than verbal contracts to avoid misunderstanding and mistrust. A written agreement not only provides protection against untimely death of one party but also facilitates an arbiter to use it in case of a conflict.

A person can engage in any business enterprise except a few that can result in social ills like selling alcohol, prostitution or selling non-kosher (*haram*) merchandise like meat of swine. This is similar to restrictions imposed in secular democracies on certain merchandise that is considered harmful to the community. The Quran directs its adherents to sell merchandise at due measure as well as receive the right quantity. Islam prohibits selling product that is not in a person's possession at the time of sale. Merchandise stocked by a manufacturer and available for delivery to the buyer is considered in possession of the seller. According to many *hadith* (saying of Prophet) a seller cannot sell food stuff unless they are in actual possession at the time of sale. This is an interesting condition considering there have been incidents when certain harmful viruses have spread through vegetables and meats creating the risk of a pandemic. Possession by a seller is meant to ensure that they are properly inspected to certify that they are free from any contamination or infection. The second reason could be to avoid speculation about food items. Condition of possession, specifically, relates to futures contracts when sales are made before a crop is harvested. These transactions are not only classified as speculation but can have an influence on the price of merchandise already available for sale. Sugar, wheat and corn are basic commodities which are traded on various exchanges around the world through futures contracts. These contracts have resulted in speculation of these basic commodities producing unnecessary price rise on many occasions.

A seller is required to provide an honest review of product specifications and should provide terms that enable a buyer to return a merchandise if it does not meet expectations or has a manufacturing defect. A merchant is expected to honor the terms of sale whether a buyer is personally present to inspect the merchandise or not.

The State as an arbiter has to ensure that transactions within its jurisdiction are conducted in the manner prescribed by the Quran. The state cannot control prices but is required to monitor the markets to prevent price gouging, artificial shortages, and monopolization. To finance its market monitoring functions the State can impose a sales tax on all merchandise except staple food that is milk, sugar, wheat, rice etc.

Business owners and managers are expected to run their businesses ethically and refrain from engaging in practices that can cause social damage. Price gouging, merchandise hoarding, environmental degradation, creating monopoly or collusion to form cartels, lobbying government to get business advantage are all prohibitive practices in an Islamic economic system.

Wealth

*(**Verse 3.180**) And let not those who covetously withhold of the gifts which Allah Hath given them of His Grace, think that it is good for them: Nay, it will be the worse for them: soon shall the things which they covetously withheld be tied to their necks Like a twisted collar, on the Day of Judgment. To Allah belongs the heritage of the heavens and the earth; and Allah is wellacquainted with all that ye do. (**Verse 3.181**) Allah hath heard the taunt of those who say: "Truly, Allah is indigent and we are rich!"- We shall certainly record their word and (their act) of slaying the prophets in defiance of right, and We shall say: "Taste ye the penalty of the Scorching Fire!*

*(**Verse 8.028**) And know ye that your possessions and your progeny are but a trial; and that it is Allah with Whom lies your highest reward.*

*(**Verse 16.071**) Allah has bestowed His gifts of sustenance more freely on some of you than on others: those more favored are not going to throw back their gifts to those whom their right hands possess, so as to be equal in that respect. Will they then deny the favors of Allah?*

*(**Verse 16.075**) Allah sets forth the Parable (of two men: one) a slave under the dominion of another; He has no power of any sort; and (the other) a man on whom We have bestowed goodly favors from Ourselves, and he spends thereof (freely), privately and publicly: are the two equal? (By no means;) praise be to Allah. But most of them understand not.*

(Verse 17.020) *Of the bounties of thy Lord We bestow freely on all- These as well as those: The bounties of thy Lord are not closed (to anyone).* ***(Verse 17.021)*** *See how We have bestowed more on some than on others; but verily the Hereafter is more in rank and gradation and more in excellence.*

(Verse 17.030) *Verily thy Lord doth provide sustenance in abundance for whom He pleaseth, and He provideth in a just measure. For He doth know and regard all His servants.*

(Verse 20.131) *Nor strain thine eyes in longing for the things We have given for enjoyment to parties of them, the splendor of the life of this world, through which We test them: but the provision of thy Lord is better and more enduring.*

(Verse 21.013) *Flee not, but return to the good things of this life which were given you, and to your homes in order that ye may be called to account.*

(Verse 24.022) *Let not those among you who are endued with grace and amplitude of means resolve by oath against helping their kinsmen, those in want, and those who have left their homes in Allah's cause: let them forgive and overlook, do you not wish that Allah should forgive you? For Allah is Oft-Forgiving, Most Merciful.*

(Verse 28.060) *The (material) things which ye are given are but the conveniences of this life and the glitter thereof; but that which is with Allah is better and more enduring: will ye not then be wise?*

(Verse 28.061) *Are (these two) alike?- one to whom We have made a goodly promise, and who is going to reach its (fulfillment), and one to whom We have given the good things of this life, but who, on the Day of Judgment, is to be among those brought up (for punishment)?*

(Verse 28.078) *He said: "This has been given to me because of a certain knowledge which I have." Did he not know that Allah had destroyed, before him, (whole) generations,- which were superior to him in strength and greater in the amount (of riches) they had collected? but the wicked are not called (immediately) to account for their sins.* ***(Verse 28.079)*** *So he went forth among his people in the (pride of his worldly) glitter. Said those whose aim is the Life of this World: "Oh! that we had the like of what Quran has got! for he is truly a lord of mighty good fortune!"* ***(Verse 28.080)*** *But those who had been granted (true) knowledge said: "Alas for you! The reward of Allah (in the Hereafter) is best for those who believe and work righteousness: but this none shall attain, save those who steadfastly persevere (in* *good)."*

(Verse 34.037) *It is not your wealth nor your sons, that will bring you nearer to Us in degree: but only those who believe and work righteousness - these are the ones for whom there is a multiplied Reward for their deeds, while secure they (reside) in the dwellings on high!*

(Verse 34.039) *Say: "Verily my Lord enlarges and restricts the Sustenance to such of his servants as He pleases: and nothing do ye spend in the least (in His cause) but He replaces it: for He is the Best of those who grant Sustenance.*

(Verse 36.047) *And when they are told, "Spend ye of (the bounties) with which Allah has provided you," the Unbelievers say to those who believe: "Shall we then feed those whom, if Allah had so willed, He would have fed, (Himself)?- Ye are in nothing but manifest error."*

(Verse 42.027) *If Allah were to enlarge the provision for His Servants, they would indeed transgress beyond all bounds through the earth; but he sends (it) down in due measure as He pleases. For He is with His Servants Well-acquainted, Watchful.*

(Verse 43.032) *Is it they who would portion out the Mercy of thy Lord? It is We Who portion out between them their livelihood in the life of this world: and We raise some of them above others in ranks, so that some may command work from others. But the Mercy of thy Lord is better than the (wealth) which they amass.*

(Verse 64.015) *Your riches and your children may be but a trial: but in the Presence of Allah, is the highest, Reward.*

(Verse 70.024) *And those in whose wealth is a recognized right.* ***(Verse 70.025)*** *For the (needy) who asks and him who is prevented (for some reason from asking);*

(Verse 74.011) *Leave Me alone, (to deal) with the (creature) whom I created (bare and) alone!-* ***(Verse 74.012)*** *To whom I granted resources in abundance,* ***(Verse 74.013)*** *And sons to be by his side!-* ***(Verse 74.014)*** *To whom I made (life) smooth and comfortable!* ***(Verse 74.015)*** *Yet is he greedy-that I should add (yet more);-* ***(Verse 74.016)*** *By no means! For to Our Signs he has been refractory!*

(Verse 100.008) *And violent is he in his love of wealth.*

(Verse 102.001) *The mutual rivalry for piling up (the good things of this world) diverts you (from the more serious things),*

(Verse 104.002) *Who pileth up wealth and layeth it by,* ***(Verse 104.003)*** *Thinking that his wealth would make him last for ever!*

In Islam wealth is considered as a blessing from God and a challenge for the person managing it. The Quran instructs that a person endowed with wealth is a trustee as at the end of temporal life all possessions are left behind and become useless. Like other spheres of social life, God provides guidance to the rich and hold them accountable for using it during life on earth. There are certain salient features of wealth management that are presented in the preceding verses and listed here:

1. A person has to spend everything beyond their means. This keeps money in circulation either through charitable causes or funding new business ventures.
2. Apart from mandatory charity *Zakat*, a wealthy person is expected to engage in *sadaqa* (voluntary charity) by contributing money as well as participate in its management as well.
3. In his will, a rich person can allocate a percentage of his inheritance to charitable causes by creating trusts and endowments.
4. In pursuit of business and wealth a person has to ensure that ethics are maintained, and no injustice is done to others.
5. Islam recognizes that there will be difference in income of people because of their abilities and inheritance. Those endowed with wealth have to do good deeds in this world to earn a reward in hereafter.
6. A wealthy citizen should not use his financial muscle to buy favors from the State officials at the expense of depriving other citizens of their rights or property.
7. A wealthy citizen should be humble and modest in his lifestyle rather than engage in extravagant spending and exhibitionism.

Foreign Relations & State Security

Foreign Relations

(Verse 3.028) *Let not the believers take for friends or helpers unbelievers rather than believers: if any do that, in nothing will there be help from Allah: except by way of precaution, that ye may guard yourselves from them. But Allah cautions you (To remember) Himself; for the final goal is to Allah.*

(Verse 3.118) *O ye who believe! Take not into your intimacy those outside your ranks: They will not fail to corrupt you. They only desire your ruin: Rank hatred has already appeared from their mouths: What their hearts conceal is far worse. We have made plain to you the Signs, if ye have wisdom.*

(Verse 4.094) *O ye who believe! When ye go abroad in the cause of Allah, investigate carefully, and say not to anyone who offers you a salutation: "Thou art none of a believer!" Coveting the perishable goods of this life: with Allah are profits and spoils abundant. Even thus were ye yourselves before, till Allah conferred on you His favors: Therefore carefully investigate. For Allah is well aware of all that ye do.*

(Verse 4.139) *Yea, to those who take for friends unbelievers rather than believers: is it honor they seek among them? Nay,- all honor is with Allah.*

(Verse 5.051) *O ye who believe! Take not the Jews and the Christians for your friends and protectors: They are but friends and protectors to each other. And he amongst you that turns to them (for friendship) is of them. Verily Allah guideth not a people unjust.*

(Verse 5.055) *Your (real) friends are (no less than) Allah, His Messenger, and the* *(fellowship of) believers,- those who establish regular prayers and regular charity, and they bow down humbly (in worship).*

(Verse 5.057) *O ye who believe! Take not for friends and protectors those who take your religion for a mockery or sport,- whether among those who received the Scripture before you, or among those who reject Faith; but fear ye Allah, if ye have faith (indeed).*

(Verse 5.082) *Strongest among men in enmity to the believers wilt thou find the Jews and*

Pagans; and nearest among them in love to the believers wilt thou find those who say, "We are Christians": because amongst these are men devoted to learning and men who have renounced the world, and they are not arrogant.

(Verse 8.058) *If thou fearest treachery from any group, throw back (their covenant) to them, (so as to be) on equal terms: for Allah loveth not the treacherous.*

(Verse 8.060) *Against them make ready your strength to the utmost of your power, including steeds of war, to strike terror into (the hearts of) the enemies, of Allah and your enemies, and others besides, whom ye may not know, but whom Allah doth know. Whatever ye shall spend in the cause of Allah, shall be repaid unto you, and ye shall not be treated unjustly.*

(Verse 9.004) *(But the treaties are) not dissolved with those Pagans with whom ye have entered into alliance and who have not subsequently failed you in aught, nor aided any one against you. So fulfill your engagements with them to the end of their term: for Allah loveth the righteous.*

(Verse 29.046) *And dispute ye not with the People of the Book, except with means better (than mere disputation), unless it be with those of them who inflict wrong (and injury): but say, "We believe in the revelation which has come down to us and in that which came down to you; Our Allah and your Allah is one; and it is to Him we bow (in Islam)."*

(Verse 49.010) *The Believers are but a single Brotherhood: So make peace and reconciliation between your two (contending) brothers; and fear Allah, that ye may receive Mercy.*

(Verse 60.001) *O ye who believe! Take not my enemies and yours as friends (or protectors),- offering them (your) love, even though they have rejected the Truth that has come to you, and have (on the contrary) driven out the Prophet and yourselves* *(from your homes), (simply) because ye believe in Allah your Lord! If ye have come out to strive in My Way and to seek My Good Pleasure, (take them not as friends), holding secret converse of love (and friendship) with them: for I know full well all that ye conceal and all that ye reveal. And any of you that does this has strayed from the Straight Path.*

Articles from the Charter of Medinah:

(14) A believer shall not slay a believer for the sake of an unbeliever, nor shall he aid an unbeliever against a believer.

(15) God's protection is one, the least of them may give protection to a stranger on their behalf. Believers are friends one to the other to the exclusion of outsiders.

(17) The peace of the believers is indivisible. No separate peace shall be made when believers are fighting in the way of God. Conditions must be fair and equitable to all.

The Treaty of Hudaybiyyah clauses 3 & 5:

(3) War activities shall be suspended for ten years, during which both parties will live in full security and neither will raise sword against the other.

(5) Whosoever to join Muhammad (Peace be upon him), or enter into treaty with him, should have the liberty to do so; and likewise whosoever wishes to join Quraish, or enter into treaty with them, should be allowed to do so.

Islam proposes that the *Ummah* (community) is linked with each other through their shared belief in one God, Prophet Mohammad (PBUH) as bearer of the message and the Quran as the guide to lead a righteous life. Islam recognizes the uniqueness of each culture and suggests organizing the community at the local level which provides legitimacy to the concept of nation state.

Islam encourages Muslim majority countries to develop inter-state relations based on following:

1. Muslim majority countries should form economic, social, security and cultural alliances. Organization of Islamic Conference (OIC) is a good platform. The Gulf Cooperation Council (GCC) is another platform, but it should not take actions and adopt resolutions that may be deemed discriminating towards non-Arab Muslim countries.

2. Unprovoked aggression should not be adopted against Christian and Jewish countries (Verse 29.046). Verse 5.051 and Verse 5.057 have been taken out of context by many writers and commentators. These verses do not suggest complete break-up of relationship with people of the book (Christians and Jews). These verses instruct that security and protection of Muslim states should be a mutual responsibility rather than relegated to others. God advises Muslims that it is better to depend on each other rather than relegate State protect to others. At the same time Muslim countries should remember that religious differences could in some cases result in violent conflicts. This scenario has played out throughout history in the form of crusades at the dawn of Islam when West retaliated to overthrow Muslim rulers of Spain and recapture Jerusalem. Later occupation of Muslim lands by Christian majority Western imperial powers created religious friction. Even after gaining independence many Muslim countries face aggression from non-Muslim countries and interference in their domestic affairs through proxy rulers. Western scholars including Samuel Huntington have presented a theory that cultural differences could produce violent struggle for access to resources and political dominance. He has suggested that Muslim majority countries could jostle for power with Christian dominated Western civilization and communist China.
3. The Quran advises Muslims that all treaties and agreements should be honored unless the other party violates it. A historical precedence is established from tradition of Prophet Mohammad (PBUH) who signed a treaty of cooperation and security with Jewish tribes in the vicinity of Medina (appendix I). When these Jewish tribes violated the terms of the agreement, in the war against the Meccans, only then did Prophet Mohammad (PBUH) cancel that pact.
4. From articles of the Treaty of Hudaybiyyah (appendix II) it is obvious that when a state is socially and economically weak, she should avoid conflict and focus on community building. Islam advises principles of prudence and pragmatism in dealing with other States rather than rash action to endanger the community.

5. The Islamic concept of *Ummah* not only requires cooperation between Muslim majority countries but also advise them to ensure that rights of Muslims, in countries where they are a minority, are protected. Rights of Muslim minorities should be part of diplomatic relations and an item of all treatises.

State Security & War

*(**Verse 2.190**) Fight in the cause of Allah those who fight you, but do not transgress limits; for Allah loveth not transgressors.*

*(**Verse 2.193**) And fight them on until there is no more tumult or oppression, and there prevail justice and faith in Allah; but if they cease, let there be no hostility except to those who practice oppression.*

***Verse 4.075**) And why should ye not fight in the cause of Allah and of those who, being weak, are ill-treated (and oppressed)?- Men, women, and children, whose cry is: "Our Lord! Rescue us from this town, whose people are oppressors; and raise for us from thee one who will protect; and raise for us from thee one who will help!" (**Verse 4.076**) Those who believe fight in the cause of Allah, and those who reject Faith fight in the cause of Evil: So fight ye against the friends of Satan: feeble indeed is the cunning of Satan. (**Verse 4.077**) Hast thou not turned Thy vision to those who were told to hold back their hands (from fight) but establish regular prayers and spend in regular charity? When (at length) the order for fighting was issued to them, behold! A section of them feared men as - or even more than - they should have feared Allah: They said: "Our Lord! Why hast Thou ordered us to fight? Wouldst Thou not Grant us respite to our (natural) term, near (enough)?" Say: "Short is the enjoyment of this world: the Hereafter is the best for those who do right: Never will ye be dealt with unjustly in the very least!*

*(**Verse 8.039**) And fight them on until there is no more tumult or oppression, and there prevail justice and faith in Allah altogether and everywhere; but if they cease, verily Allah doth see all that they do.*

*(**Verse 8.057**) If ye gain the mastery over them in war, disperse, with them, those who follow them, that they may remember. (**Verse 8.058**) If thou fearest treachery from any group, throw back (their covenant) to them, (so as to be) on equal terms: for*

Allah loveth not the treacherous. ***(Verse 8.059)*** *Let not the unbelievers think that they can get the better (of the godly): they will never frustrate (them).* ***(Verse 8.060)*** *Against them make ready your strength to the utmost of your power, including steeds of war, to strike terror into (the hearts of) the enemies, of Allah and your enemies, and others besides, whom ye may not know, but whom Allah doth know. Whatever ye shall spend in the cause of Allah, shall be repaid unto you, and ye shall not be treated unjustly.* ***(Verse 8.061)*** *But if the enemy incline towards peace, do thou (also) incline towards peace, and trust in Allah: for He is One that heareth and knoweth (all things).* ***(Verse 8.062)*** *Should they intend to deceive thee,- verily Allah sufficeth thee: He it is That hath strengthened thee with His aid and with (the company of) the Believers;*

(Verse 9.029) *Fight those who believe not in Allah nor the Last Day, nor hold that forbidden which hath been forbidden by Allah and His Messenger, nor acknowledge the religion of Truth, (even if they are) of the People of the Book, until they pay the Jizya with willing submission, and feel themselves subdued.*

(Verse 22.039) *To those against whom war is made, permission is given (to fight), because they are wronged;- and verily, Allah is most powerful for their aid;-* ***(Verse 22.040)*** *(They are) those who have been expelled from their homes in defiance of right,- (for no cause) except that they say, "our Lord is Allah". Did not Allah check one set of people by means of another, there would surely have been pulled down monasteries, churches, synagogues, and mosques, in which the name of Allah is commemorated in abundant measure. Allah will certainly aid those who aid his (cause);- for verily Allah is full of Strength, Exalted in Might, (able to enforce His Will).*

(Verse 42.039) *And those who, when an oppressive wrong is inflicted on them, (are not cowed but) help and defend themselves.*

(Verse 60.008) *Allah forbids you not, with regard to those who fight you not for (your) Faith nor drive you out of your homes, from dealing kindly and justly with them: for Allah loveth those who are just.* ***(Verse 60.009)*** *Allah only forbids you, with regard to those who fight you for (your) Faith, and drive you out of your homes, and support (others) in driving you out, from turning to them (for friendship and protection). It is such as turn to them (in these circumstances), that do wrong.*

Treaty of Hudaybiyyah clauses 3 & 5:

(3) War activities shall be suspended for ten years, during which both parties will live in full security and neither will raise sword against the other.

(5) Whosoever to join Muhammad (Peace be upon him), or enter into treaty with him, should have the liberty to do so; and likewise whosoever wishes to join Quraish, or enter into treaty with them, should be allowed to do so.

The preceding verses provide a good understanding of the concept of war in an Islamic Social State:

1. War is only justified in response to aggression or oppression.
2. Treaties and covenants should be respected in times of war unless they are abrogated by the other party.
3. Muslim majority countries should collaborate with each other in security pacts to ensure protection against aggression.
4. Security of an Islamic State is ensured when it is always prepared for war in terms of weapons and training.
5. The Treaty of Hudaybiyyah provides a good example from the tradition of Prophet Mohammad (PBUH) that if a treaty ensures peace and stability then it is preferred over war.
6. The Islamic Social State has to concern itself with the well being and security of its citizens first before she considers waging war to protect others.

Islamic concept of war is defensive. Amir ul Muluk (President) of the State, elected by the people, has the executive authority to declare war after consultation with his cabinet the constitution may require that *Majlis-e-Shura* has to approve the declaration and provisions for war efforts to create balance of power. Approval of *Majlis-e-Shura* to declare war provides a safety valve to ensure that interests of a community are not risked by the decision of few. No other entity, civic or religious, has the authority to independently announce a war or uprising. The Quran instructs that once a war is declared there should be no ceasefire until the oppressor is defeated and signs a peace treaty ensuring future safety and security of community. All citizens of the State that are healthy are required to offer their services in times of war when called on by the State.

Al-Tabari reports first Caliph Abu Bakr addressing a departing army about the conduct of war in these words:

"O people! I charge you with ten rules; learn them well!

Do not betray, or misappropriate any part of the booty; do not practice treachery or mutilation. Do not kill a young child, an old man, or a woman. Do not uproot or burn palms or cut down fruit trees. Do not slaughter a sheep or a cow or a camel, except for food. You will meet people who have set themselves apart in hermitages; leave them to accomplish the purpose for which they have done this. You will come upon people who will bring you dishes with various kinds of foods. If you partake of them, pronounce God's name over what you eat. You will meet people who have shaved the crown of their heads, leaving a band of hair around it. Strike them with the sword. Go in God's name, and may God protect you from sword and pestilence."

(Islam, Volume I, Bernard Lewis, page 213)

Appendix I

THE CHARTER OF MEDINAH
622 C.E.

In the name of God, the Compassionate, the Merciful.

(1) This is a document from Muhammad the prophet (governing the relations) between the believers and Muslims of Quraysh and Yathrib, and those who followed them and joined them and labored with them.

(2) They are one community (umma) to the exclusion of all men.

(3) The Quraysh emigrants according to their present custom shall pay the bloodwit within their number and shall redeem their prisoners with the kindness and justice common among believers.

(4-8) The B. 'Auf according to their present custom shall pay the bloodwit they paid in heatheism; every section shall redeem its prisoners with the kindness and justice common among believers. The B. Sa ida, the B. 'l-Harith, and the B. Jusham, and the B. al-Najjar likewise.

(9-11) The B. 'Amr b. 'Auf, the B. al-Nabit and the B. al-'Aus likewise.

(12)(a) Believers shall not leave anyone destitute among them by not paying his redemption money or bloodwit in kindness.

(12)(b) A believer shall not take as an ally the freedman of another Muslim against him.

(13) The God-fearing believers shall be against the rebellious or him who seeks to spread injustice, or sin or animosity, or corruption between believers; the hand of every man shall be against him even if he be a son of one of them.

(14) A believer shall not slay a believer for the sake of an unbeliever, nor shall he aid an unbeliever against a believer.

(15) God's protection is one, the least of them may give protection to a stranger on their behalf. Believers are friends one to the other to the exclusion of outsiders.

(16) To the Jew who follows us belong help and equality. He shall not be wronged nor shall his enemies be aided.

(17) The peace of the believers is indivisible. No separate peace shall be made when believers are fighting in the way of God. Conditions must be fair and equitable to all.

(18) In every foray a rider must take another behind him.

(19) The believers must avenge the blood of one another shed in the way of God.

(20)(a) The God-fearing believers enjoy the best and most upright guidance.

(20)(b) No polytheist shall take the property of person of Quraysh under his protection nor shall he intervene against a believer.

(21) Whoever is convicted of killing a believer without good reason shall be subject to retaliation unless the next of kin is satisfied (with blood-money), and the believers shall be against him as one man, and they are bound to take action against him.

(22) It shall not be lawful to a believer who holds by what is in this document and believes in God and the last day to help an evil-doer or to shelter him. The curse of God and His anger on the day of resurrection will be upon him if he does, and neither repentance nor ransom will be received from him.

(23) Whenever you differ about a matter it must be referred to God and to Muhammad.

(24) The Jews shall contribute to the cost of war so long as they are fighting alongside the believers.

(25) The Jews of the B. 'Auf are one community with the believers (the Jews have their religion and the Muslims have theirs), their freedmen and their persons except those who behave unjustly and sinfully, for they hurt but themselves and their families.

(26-35) The same applies to the Jews of the B. al-Najjar, B. al-Harith, B. Sai ida, B. Jusham, B. al-Aus, B. Tha'laba, and the Jafna, a clan of the Tha'laba and the B. alShutayba. Loyalty is a protection against treachery. The freedmen of

Tha 'laba are as themselves. The close friends of the Jews are as themselves.

(36) None of them shall go out to war save the permission of Muhammad, but he shall not be prevented from taking revenge for a wound. He who slays a man without warning slays himself and his household, unless it be one who has wronged him, for God will accept that.

(37)The Jews must bear their expenses and the Muslims their expenses. Each must help the other against anyone who attacks the people of this document. They must seek mutual advice and consultation, and loyalty is a protection against treachery. A man is not liable for his ally's misdeeds. The wronged must be helped.

(38) The Jews must pay with the believers so long as war lasts.

(39) Yathrib shall be a sanctuary for the people of this document.

(40) A stranger under protection shall be as his host doing no harm and committing no crime.

(41) A woman shall only be given protection with the consent of her family.

(42) If any dispute or controversy likely to cause trouble should arise it must be referred to God and to Muhammad the apostle of God. God accepts what is nearest to piety and goodness in this document.

(43) Quraysh and their helpers shall not be given protection.

(44) The contracting parties are bound to help one another against any attack on Yathrib.

(45)(a) If they are called to make peace and maintain it they must do so; and if they make a similar demand on the Muslims it must be carried out except in the case of a holy war.

(45)(b) Every one shall have his portion from the side to which he belongs.

(46) The Jews of al-Aus, their freedmen and themselves have the same standing with the people of this document in purely loyalty from the people of this document. Loyalty is a protection against treachery. He who acquires ought acquires it for himself. God approves of this document.

(47) This deed will not protect the unjust and the sinner. The man who goes forth to fight and the man who stays at home in the city is safe unless he has been unjust and sinned. God is the protector of the good and God-fearing man and Muhammad is the apostle of God.

Appendix II

THE TREATY OF HUDAYBIYYAH
628 AD

The clauses of the said treaty go as follows:

1. The Muslims shall return this time and come back next year, but they shall not stay in Makkah for more than three days.
2. They shall not come back armed but can bring with them swords only sheathed in scabbards and these shall be kept in bags.
3. War activities shall be suspended for ten years, during which both parties will live in full security and neither will raise sword against the other.
4. If anyone from Quraish goes over to Muhammad (Peace be upon him) without his guardian's permission, he should be sent back to Quraish, but should any of Muhammad's followers to Quraish, he shall not be sent back.
5. Whosoever to join Muhammad (Peace be upon him), or enter into treaty with him, should have the liberty to do so; and likewise whosoever wishes to join Quraish, or enter into treaty with them, should be allowed to do so.

Appendix III

Last Hajj Sermon of Prophet Mohammad (PBUH)

(This Sermon was delivered on the Ninth Day of Dhul Hijjah 10 A.H or 9th March 632 CE in the Uranah Valley of mount Arafat)

"O People, lend me an attentive ear, for I know not whether after this year, I shall ever be amongst you again. Therefore listen to what I am saying to you very carefully and TAKE THESE WORDS TO THOSE WHO COULD NOT BE PRESENT HERE TODAY.

O People, just as you regard this month, this day, this city as Sacred, so regard the life and property of every Muslim as a sacred trust. Return the goods entrusted to you to their rightful owners. Hurt no one so that no one may hurt you. Remember that you will indeed meet your LORD, and that HE will indeed reckon your deeds. ALLAH has forbidden you to take usury (interest), therefore all interest obligation shall henceforth be waived. Your capital, however, is yours to keep. You will neither inflict nor suffer any inequity. Allah has Judged that there shall be no interest and that all the interest due to Abbas ibn 'Abd'al Muttalib (Prophet's uncle) shall henceforth be waived...

Beware of Satan, for the safety of your religion. He has lost all hope that he will ever be able to lead you astray in big things, so beware of following him in small things.

O People, it is true that you have certain rights with regard to your women, but they also have rights over you. Remember that you have taken them as your wives only under Allah's trust and with His permission. If they abide by your right then to them belongs the right to be fed and clothed in kindness.

Do treat your women well and be kind to them for they are your partners and committed helpers. And it is your right that they do not make friends with any one of whom you do not approve, as well as never to be unchaste.

O People, listen to me in earnest, worship ALLAH, say your five daily prayers (Salah), fast during the month of Ramadan, and give your wealth in Zakat. Perform Hajj if you can afford to.

All mankind is from Adam and Eve, an Arab has no superiority over a non-Arab nor a non-Arab has any superiority over an Arab; also a white has no superiority over black nor a black has any superiority over white except by piety and good action. Learn that every Muslim is a brother to every Muslim and that the Muslims constitute one brotherhood. Nothing shall be legitimate to a Muslim which belongs to a fellow Muslim unless it was given freely and willingly. Do not, therefore, do injustice to yourselves.

Remember, one day you will appear before ALLAH and answer your deeds. So beware, do not stray from the path of righteousness after I am gone.

O People, NO PROPHET OR APOSTLE WILL COME AFTER ME AND NO NEW FAITH WILL BE BORN. Reason well, therefore, O People, and understand words which I convey to you. I leave behind me two things, the QURAN and my example, the SUNNAH and if you follow these you will never go astray.

All those who listen to me shall pass on my words to others and those to others again; and may the last ones understand my words better than those who listen to me directly. Be my witness, O ALLAH, that I have conveyed your message to your people".

Source URL: http://www.islamicity.com/Mosque/lastserm.htm

Selected List for further reading

- Esposito, John L., *Islam and Politics*, 4th Edition, Syracuse University Press, 1998
- Watt, W. Montgomery, *Islamic Political Thought*, Edinburgh at the University Press, 1968
- Maududi, Sayyid Abul A'la, *Islamic Law and Constitution*, 13th Edition, Islamic Publications (Pvt.) Ltd., 2005
- Graham, Major General George Farquhar Irving, *The life and Work of Sir Syed Ahmed Khan*, Oxford University Press, Karachi, Pakistan, 1974
- Khaldun, Ibn, *The Muqaddimah*, translation by Franz Roenthal, Princeton University Press, 2005
- Qutub, Sayyid, *Social Justice in Islam*, translated by John B. Hardie, Islamic Publications International, 2000
- Rahman, Fazlur, *Major themes of the Quran*, The University of Chicago Press, 1989
- Rahman, Fazlur, *Islam & Modernity*, The University of Chicago Press, 1982
- Rahman, Fazlur , *Islam*, 2nd edition, University of Chicago Press, 2002
- Shugart, Matthew Soberg and Carey, John M, *Presidents and Assemblies, Constitutional Design and Electoral Dynamics*, Cambridge University Press, 1995
- Iqbal, Allama Muhammad, *The reconstruction of Religious Thought in Islam*, 4th Edition, Ilm-o-irfan Publishers, Lahore, Pakistan, 2003
- Hathout, Hassan, *Reading the Muslim Mind*, American Trust Publications,

1995

- Armstrong, Karen, *A History of God*, Ballantine Books, New York, 1993
- Moin, Baqer, Khomeini, *Life of the Ayatollah*, Thomas Dunne Books, New York, 2000
- Keddie, Nikki R., *Sayyid Jama ad-din Afghani*, a political biography, University of California Press, 1972
- Keddie, Nikki R, *An Islamic Response to Imperialism*, Political and Religious writings of Sayyid Jamal ad-Din "Al-Afghani", 1968, University of California Press
- Sharif, M.M., A History of Muslim Philosophy, Volume I, Pakistan Philosophical Congress, 1963
- Sharif, M.M., A History of Muslim Philosophy, Volume II, Pakistan Philosophical Congress, 1966
- Charles E. Butterworth, *AlFarabi- The political writings*, Cornell University Press, 2001
- Khan, M.A. Muqtedar, *Islamic Democratic Discourse, Theory, Debates, and Philosophical Perspectives*, Lexington Books, 2006
- Sadri, Mahmoud & Sadri, *Ahmad, Reasons, Freedom & Democracy in Islam*, Essential Writings of 'AbdolKarim Soroush', Oxford University Press, 2000
- Black, Anthony, *The History of Islamic Political Thought*, Routledge, 2001
- Ebaugh, Helen Rose, *The Gulen Movement*, Springer, 2010
- An-Naim, Abdullah Ahmed, *Islam and the Secular State: Negotiating the future of Shari'a*, Harvard University Press, 2008
- El-Hibri, Tayeb, Parable and Politics in Early Islamic History, The Rashidun Caliphs, Columbia University Press, 2010
- Lewis, Bernard, Islam- from the Prophet Mohammad to the Capture of Constantinople, Volume I & II, Walker and Company, 1974
- Mahdi, Muhsin S., Alfarabi and the Foundation of Islamic Political Philosophy, The University of Chicago Press, 2001

About the Author

Abdul Quayyum Khan Kundi is known for his contributions to Pakistani newspapers through op-ed columns. He has shared his insights on a wide range of topics including politics, social issues, and foreign policy. His writing has appeared in prominent publications such as Independent Urdu, The Daily Times, The Frontier Post, and Pakistan Today.

In a particular op-ed column dated December 14, 2011, Mr. Kundi discussed the emergence of a new multi-polar world order. He argued that American hegemony was being challenged by a collaborative effort between China and Russia, leading to the development of a new cold war scenario. This topic reflects his engagement with global geopolitics and international relations.

Mr. Kundi has also authored several books that delve into various subjects. His first book, "Freedom by Choice," is a compilation of writings that explore US-Pakistan relations, reforms in the Muslim world, and the balance of power in South Asia. This book showcases his keen interest in diplomacy and regional dynamics.

"Lessons from the Quran," his second book, focuses on Quranic verses with an emphasis on their relevance to social values. This work highlights his engagement with religious and ethical matters.

His book titled "Islamic Social Contract" is a significant effort to propose a political system rooted in the social values outlined in the Quran and the Sunnah (tradition) of the Prophet Mohammad (PBUH). Mr. Kundi believes that the Muslim world's political liberation can only be achieved by developing systems that align with Islamic cultural traditions. This book offers a framework for building stable societies, drawing from the context of reform movements like the "Arab Spring."

Finally, his book "Thoughts" is a collection of metaphysical speculations covering topics related to religion, philosophy, and science. This work reflects his intellectual curiosity and willingness to explore abstract and philosophical ideas.

In summary, Abdul Quayyum Khan Kundi is a multifaceted thinker and writer who has made contributions to the discussion of politics, religion, and global affairs, particularly within the context of Pakistan and the Muslim world.

You can connect with me on:

- http://abdulqkundi.com
- https://twitter.com/aqkkundi
- http://facebook.com/abdul.quayyum.khan.kundi
- https://youtube.com/@AbdulQuayyumKhanKundi

Subscribe to my newsletter:

https://books2read.com/author/abdul-quayyum-khan-kundi/subscribe/59408

Also by Abdul Kundi

Thoughts: God, Science, & Human Nature
Religion, philosophy, and science sometimes appear to contradict each other. The deeper reality is that these operate in tandem to provide a holistic appreciation of life. Emotional crisis and physical trauma invoke questions about the purpose of life, humanity, and our place in the universe. We need to reconnect with our soul and be comfortable with the nature of things. This book is an effort to help make sense of life and our place in it.

Legacy of the Third Way: A Novel
One man's struggle against the system.

A coming of age, fictional biographical, and historical fiction novel. Releasing spring 2024.

Milton Keynes UK
Ingram Content Group UK Ltd.
UKHW011051240124
436611UK00004B/149

9 798869 011596